Inside the Ancient World

ROMAN SOCIETY

INSIDE THE ANCIENT WORLD
General Editor: Michael Gunningham

The following titles are available in this series:

*Denotes books which are especially suited to GCSE or studies at a comparable 16+ level. The remainder may be useful at that level, but can also be used by students on more advanced courses.

Inside the Ancient World

ROMAN SOCIETY

David Taylor

BRISTOL CLASSICAL PRESS

General Editor: Michael Gunningham

First published by Macmillan Education Ltd, 1980
Published by Thomas Nelson and Sons Ltd, 1992

Published in 1997 by Bristol Classical Press
an imprint of
Gerald Duckworth & Co. Ltd
61 Frith Street
London W1V 5TA

Reprinted 1999

A catalogue record for this book is available
from the British Library

ISBN 1-85399-553-3

Printed in Great Britain by
Antony Rowe Ltd

Contents

Illustrations

n street

ore spectacular, and certainly better known, are Pompeii and
um. When the volcano Vesuvius erupted in August AD 79,
s were completely buried – Pompeii suffered a hail of ash
, Herculaneum a tidal stream of molten lava which prevail-
bore swiftly towards the doomed town, covering it twelve
p with a substance as hard as concrete. Herculaneum
haeologists with a formidable task, especially as a modern
na, now occupies much of the site. But the preservation of
s is remarkable: many houses are still in almost perfect
At Pompeii, where looters and treasure-seekers ransacked
ings, archaeologists have now uncovered three-fifths of the
excavations provide an opportunity to study Roman life
ar moment: the late first century AD.
like Britain and France add their own contribution. No
ptions produced a wreck like Pompeii, pathetic and
But archaeologists have found numerous country houses
traces of Roman occupation survive in many towns. In
-names ending in -cester, -chester or -caster (from cas-
show a former Roman settlement, often with remains of
or other buildings. Around Hadrian's Wall, in an area
uninhabited, Roman forts have recently been excavated,
urope similar archaeological work continues.

Author's Note

To attempt to condense such vast topics into so small a span is vastly
impudent, and a word of apology for the numerous short-cuts is
essential – in particular, for the practice of quoting only brief extracts,
sometimes with major excisions, from the ancient authors. This drastic
treatment – employed solely because of shortage of space – is partly
defensible on the grounds that there are readily accessible editions and
translations of all the major writers cited. In translating passages, I
have been guided primarily by the aims of immediacy and intelligibility.

Deepest gratitude is due to Mr L. K. Turner, Headmaster of
Watford GS, to Herts County Council and above all to the Warden
and Fellows of Merton College, Oxford, who generously provided me
with *otium cum luxuria* for carrying out research into the subject,
during Hilary Term 1978; also to my wife for valuable assistance with
choice of extracts and illustrations; finally, to Mr Thomas Braun (Dean
of Merton College, Oxford) for wise advice and scholarly interest in
the work, for his careful reading of the manuscript, and for his many
helpful suggestions. None of the above can take any blame for what
remains.

Acknowledgements

The author and publishers wish to acknowledge the following photograph sources:

Ronald Sheridan Fig 1; Mansell Collection Figs 2, 3, 5, 6, 10, 11, 12,
15, 16, 17, 18, 19, 21; Museo Nationale, Napoli Fig 4; Ashmolean
Museum, Oxford Fig 9; German Arch. Inst., Rome Fig 13; Victoria &
Albert Museum Fig 14.

The publishers have made every effort to trace the copyright holders,
but if they have inadvertently overlooked any they will be pleased to
make the necessary arrangements at the ealiest opportunity.

Important Dates

Roman Society lasted over a thousand years, but this book focuses on a period of about two hundred years – from approximately the death of Julius Caesar to AD150. The relatively slow social change at Rome (compared, say, with the period from the eighteenth to twentieth centuries in our own society) enables us to present a picture of a society which was largely stable in customs and lifestyle. But a frozen image is still over-simplified; at times, therefore, it has been useful to look backwards to the Republican world or forward to later emperors in order to indicate particularly marked areas of change. The following list of dates provides the basic framework in which the book operates.

Timechart

Roman Emperors		Important writers	
27 BC–AD 14	Augustus (Octavian)	Catullus	(c.87–54 BC)
AD 14–37	Tiberius	Lucretius	(94–55 BC)
AD 37–41	Caligula (Gaius)	Caesar	(c.100–44 BC)
AD 41–54	Claudius	Cicero	(106–43 BC)
AD 54–68	Nero	Varro	(116–27 BC)
AD 68-69	Galba	Livy	(c.59 BC–AD 17)
AD 69	Otho	Virgil	(70–19 BC)
AD 69	Vitellius	Horace	(65–8 BC)
AD 69–79	Vespasian	Ovid	(43 BC–AD 17)
AD 79–81	Titus	Seneca	(c.4 BC–AD 65)
AD 81–96	Domitian	Petronius	(?1st C. AD)
AD 96–98	Nerva	Pliny the Elder	(AD 23–79)
AD 98–117	Trajan	Martial	(AD c.40–104)
AD 117–138	Hadrian	Tacitus	(AD c.56–115)
		Pliny the Younger	(AD c.61–112)
		Juvenal	(AD c.60–127)
		Suetonius	(AD c.69–130)
		Plutarch	(AD c.50–120)

1
How do we know [...] Roman Societ[...]

Time-travellers can be whisked speedily from [...] another, covering thousands of years in no ti[...] part in the lives of people of completely differ[...] ately, they are characters from fiction. Other [...] vision. They can see only what surrounds th[...] If they wish, for example, to study the lives [...] America in the first century AD, they wil[...] information. So why should things be diffe[...] period of history? The answer lies in the va[...] This is of different kinds, none of which nee[...] time-traveller.

Types of evidence

FROM TOWNS

From all over Rome's empire, stretching f[...] Africa, Roman buildings and even town[...] ists are constantly making fresh discover[...]

When the site of a town has been re-u[...] only discover remains if an area is cleare[...] Roman town of Londinium (London) h[...] know its main outline and the sites of [...] have not been re-occupied. Timgad, in [...] neglected since the Romans moved ou[...] after the Roman irrigation-system h[...] remarkably vivid impression of a ghos[...] harbour-town, Ostia, twenty-five kilo[...] Tiber. But while Rome has been inh[...] largely ignored because the site was i[...] began in the nineteenth century and [...] many of the town's buildings are ag[...]

A Pompei[...]

Even m[...] Herculane[...] both tow[...] and stone[...] ing winds [...] metres de[...] presents a[...] town, Resi[...] its building[...] condition. [...] many build[...] town. Thes[...] at a particu[...]

Countrie[...] volcanic er[...] spectacular. [...] (*villae*), and[...] Britain place[...] *trum*, a fort[...] Roman walls[...] now largely [...] and all over [...]

10

HOUSE-CONTENTS

Buildings are not empty shells – they contain numerous objects. To appreciate the importance of these, think how much more a future archaeologist could discover about our society from examining full houses rather than empty ones. Here Pompeii and Herculaneum are especially helpful. Some wooden pieces of furniture (usually the first items to perish) have been preserved, carbonised like a form of coal. Interior decoration, cutlery and crockery survive – even plates of food which there was no time to eat.

LITERATURE

Unlike many ancient and some modern societies, Romans could write – many of them ordinary people, as well as the highly-educated. Much Roman literature, both poetry and prose, has survived until today, copied out in monasteries and preserved in libraries. The Renaissance (re-birth) of the fourteenth and fifteenth centuries saw great interest in these writings, and European scholars continued to communicate in Latin until much later. Roman literature was and still is studied in schools and universities.

OTHER WRITING

Towns and houses also provide written evidence. At Pompeii, excavators found the full financial and personal records of the banker Lucius Caecilius Iucundus, in a safe in his house. Inscriptions of various kinds were written on walls, tombstones, pillars or pieces of furniture: public records and electioneering slogans, poems and messages to lovers. There are official and dignified pieces of writing by professional sign-writers, and personal and informal messages, scratched with red chalk or nails by amateur graffiti-writers.

GAPS IN THE EVIDENCE

The picture is not complete. Today's historians, sociologists and anthropologists rely heavily on statistics to work out population-size, or the number of children per family, but this did not apply to the Romans. Scholars can only make intelligent guesses, based on fragmentary information. Also, we have little written by women, children, slaves or poor men, apart from some graffiti and inscriptions. A book like this, therefore, must have gaps. But it should be clear that the quest is not hopeless.

2
Town life

Domus and insula

Roman towns and cities contained two basic types of home. The *domus* was a private, self-contained town house, usually inhabited by a single household (the master, his immediate family and dependants – slaves and freedmen); rooms were sometimes let to tenants. The *insula* (literally 'island') was a block surrounded by streets, containing a number of flats or apartments. The *domus* was a one- or at most two-storey building; an *insula* could have several floors.

Except for literary references, evidence of private houses at Rome is scanty. We know that they were for a privileged few. A thorough survey from the fourth century AD records 1,797 private houses and 46,602 *insulae* – housing an estimated population of around 1½ million. The city had expanded since the first century AD, when about a thousand families out of a total population of one million lived in private houses. There was a great gulf between this select minority and the rest, who lived in rented accommodation in the *insulae*.

PUBLIC SPLENDOUR...

The contrast was reflected in the mixture of grand public buildings in marble and the *insulae* in their narrow streets. Public buildings were a symbol of Rome's imperial power. Augustus claimed that he found Rome a city of brick and turned it into a city of marble, but this never really applied to the flat-dwelling crowds. Rome's temples, of which the city had many, embodied the public splendour. They often adjoined a *forum*, originally a market-square. Although shops and stalls continued, the *forum* also became a civic centre. As well as temples there were law-courts and offices; shady colonnades (covered paths, with rows of pillars), where people could relax, ran round the sides. The central *forum* was *Forum Romanum*, but emperors added others. The largest and most magnificent was begun by Trajan and completed by his successor Hadrian. Three hundred years later, the

Romans appointed an emperor who had never been to Rome. He was Constantius, and this was his reaction:

When he arrived at Trajan's *Forum*, a construction unique in the whole world, in our view, and wonderful even in the eyes of the gods, he was rooted to the spot in astonishment; he turned his attention throughout the gigantic complex, which no story-teller could describe and no mortal imitate.

[Ammianus Marcellinus, XVI 10 15]

AND PRIVATE SQUALOR

Rome's literature often emphasises how unpleasant and unsafe *insulae* could be. The city never fully solved the lack of space. As in modern Hong Kong, when an expanding population could not be accommodated by spreading outwards into suburbs, buildings were raised ever higher. Cicero wrote that 'Rome was raised high and suspended in the air on its *cenacula* [the flats inside an *insula*]'. Roman builders did not always ensure that buildings could support the extra height. There was much 'jerry-building', with landlords profiting from the insecurity of *insulae*. One was the wealthy Crassus:

Crassus used to buy slaves who were architects or builders. When he had more than five hundred, he bought up buildings which were on fire, and those adjoining them – getting a low price because of owners' fear and uncertainty. Thus he gained possession of a vast area in Rome.

[Plutarch, *Life of Crassus* 2]

The slaves then built new *insulae* on the sites of the destroyed buildings, and Crassus charged high rents for basic accommodation.

Augustus attempted to do something about poor building standards and the risks of city-life:

As far as human agency could, he made the city safe for the future . . . He instituted nightly guards and regular watches against fires, and to check floods he widened and cleared the channel of the Tiber, which had been blocked with debris and projecting buildings. [Suetonius, *Life of Augustus* 30]

He also introduced a law restricting the height of *insulae* to twenty metres, (about six storeys). But this proved almost impossible to enforce, and control was never completely effective. The poet Martial talks of climbing two hundred steps to a tiny garret, and, even allowing for poetic licence, high and dangerous blocks certainly continued to exist.

The House of Diana today. (In the picture can be seen some twentieth-century women)

INSULAE AT OSTIA

Literary evidence suggests that individual flats were often tiny, dark places with one room housing a whole family. But as no *insulae* from Rome survive, it is necessary to look at those from Ostia, where the overspill population from Rome led to rapid expansion.

Builders who had purchased the land naturally wanted the maximum return for their investment, so space was used as fully as possible. *Insulae* normally had at least three storeys, with access to upper floors from staircases leading directly from the streets. The picture shows the *insula* known as the House of Diana. This was semi-detached; only two walls faced the street; the others were blocked by buildings, with no doors or windows. The central courtyard was therefore essential to admit light; windows in outer walls were often only wooden shutters, but the Romans also used selenite, a material far less transparent than glass.

Individual rooms had no private water-supply, and residents drew water from a cistern in the courtyard. Other *insulae* lacked even this, and tenants used tanks in the streets to which water was piped from aqueducts.

The House of Diana was about thirty-nine by twenty-three metres,

Author's Note

To attempt to condense such vast topics into so small a span is vastly impudent, and a word of apology for the numerous short-cuts is essential – in particular, for the practice of quoting only brief extracts, sometimes with major excisions, from the ancient authors. This drastic treatment – employed solely because of shortage of space – is partly defensible on the grounds that there are readily accessible editions and translations of all the major writers cited. In translating passages, I have been guided primarily by the aims of immediacy and intelligibility.

Deepest gratitude is due to Mr L. K. Turner, Headmaster of Watford GS, to Herts County Council and above all to the Warden and Fellows of Merton College, Oxford, who generously provided me with *otium cum luxuria* for carrying out research into the subject, during Hilary Term 1978; also to my wife for valuable assistance with choice of extracts and illustrations; finally, to Mr Thomas Braun (Dean of Merton College, Oxford) for wise advice and scholarly interest in the work, for his careful reading of the manuscript, and for his many helpful suggestions. None of the above can take any blame for what remains.

Acknowledgements

The author and publishers wish to acknowledge the following photograph sources:

Ronald Sheridan Fig 1; Mansell Collection Figs 2, 3, 5, 6, 10, 11, 12, 15, 16, 17, 18, 19, 21; Museo Nationale, Napoli Fig 4; Ashmolean Museum, Oxford Fig 9; German Arch. Inst., Rome Fig 13; Victoria & Albert Museum Fig 14.

Important Dates

Roman Society lasted over a thousand years, but this book focuses on a period of about two hundred years – from approximately the death of Julius Caesar to AD150. The relatively slow social change at Rome (compared, say, with the period from the eighteenth to twentieth centuries in our own society) enables us to present a picture of a society which was largely stable in customs and lifestyle. But a frozen image is still over-simplified; at times, therefore, it has been useful to look backwards to the Republican world or forward to later emperors in order to indicate particularly marked areas of change. The following list of dates provides the basic framework in which the book operates.

Timechart

Roman Emperors

27 BC–AD	14	Augustus (Octavian)
AD	14–37	Tiberius
AD	37–41	Caligula (Gaius)
AD	41–54	Claudius
AD	54–68	Nero
AD	68–69	Galba ·
AD	69	Otho
AD	69	Vitellius
AD	69–79	Vespasian
AD	79–81	Titus
AD	81–96	Domitian
AD	96–98	Nerva
AD	98–117	Trajan
AD	117–138	Hadrian

Important writers

Catullus	(c.87–54 BC)
Lucretius	(94–55 BC)
Caesar	(c.100–44 BC)
Cicero	(106–43 BC)
Varro	(116–27 BC)
Livy	(c.59 BC–AD 17)
Virgil	(70–19 BC)
Horace	(65–8 BC)
Ovid	(43 BC–AD 17)
Seneca	(c.4 BC–AD 65)
Petronius	(?1st C. AD)
Pliny the Elder	(AD 23–79)
Martial	(AD c.40–104)
Tacitus	(AD c.56–115)
Pliny the Younger	(AD c.61–112)
Juvenal	(AD c.60–127)
Suetonius	(AD c.69–130)
Plutarch	(AD c.50–120)

1
How do we know about Roman Society?

Time-travellers can be whisked speedily from one period of history to another, covering thousands of years in no time at all. They can take part in the lives of people of completely different societies. Unfortunately, they are characters from fiction. Other people have more limited vision. They can see only what surrounds them in their own lifetime. If they wish, for example, to study the lives of people living in North America in the first century AD, they will find a lack of detailed information. So why should things be different in Rome at the same period of history? The answer lies in the variety of evidence available. This is of different kinds, none of which needs the amazing powers of a time-traveller.

Types of evidence

FROM TOWNS

From all over Rome's empire, stretching from Britain to Asia, Spain to Africa, Roman buildings and even towns have survived. Archaeologists are constantly making fresh discoveries.

When the site of a town has been re-used in later periods, they may only discover remains if an area is cleared for a new building. Thus the Roman town of Londinium (London) has almost disappeared, but we know its main outline and the sites of some buildings. Other towns have not been re-occupied. Timgad, in North Africa, has simply stood neglected since the Romans moved out; the town was uninhabitable after the Roman irrigation-system broke down. It now gives a remarkably vivid impression of a ghost town. The city of Rome had a harbour-town, Ostia, twenty-five kilometres away at the mouth of the Tiber. But while Rome has been inhabited continuously, Ostia was largely ignored because the site was infected with malaria. Excavations began in the nineteenth century and the work has continued, so that many of the town's buildings are again visible.

A Pompeian street

Even more spectacular, and certainly better known, are Pompeii and Herculaneum. When the volcano Vesuvius erupted in August AD 79, both towns were completely buried – Pompeii suffered a hail of ash and stones, Herculaneum a tidal stream of molten lava which prevailing winds bore swiftly towards the doomed town, covering it twelve metres deep with a substance as hard as concrete. Herculaneum presents archaeologists with a formidable task, especially as a modern town, Resina, now occupies much of the site. But the preservation of its buildings is remarkable: many houses are still in almost perfect condition. At Pompeii, where looters and treasure-seekers ransacked many buildings, archaeologists have now uncovered three-fifths of the town. These excavations provide an opportunity to study Roman life at a particular moment: the late first century AD.

Countries like Britain and France add their own contribution. No volcanic eruptions produced a wreck like Pompeii, pathetic and spectacular. But archaeologists have found numerous country houses (*villae*), and traces of Roman occupation survive in many towns. In Britain place-names ending in *-cester*, *-chester* or *-caster* (from *castrum*, a fort) show a former Roman settlement, often with remains of Roman walls or other buildings. Around Hadrian's Wall, in an area now largely uninhabited, Roman forts have recently been excavated, and all over Europe similar archaeological work continues.

with four or five floors, although the top of the block has been destroyed. It is not always obvious how each room was used, but one large room was clearly the lavatory, probably shared by all tenants. Some apartments were on two or more floors, or rooms were linked by inter-connecting doors. Arrangements were flexible. Sometimes it was convenient to split flats for single tenants; at others, to keep rooms together for a family. Not all tenants were long-term residents; renting by the month was common.

As in other insulae at Ostia, several rooms were spacious, with good lighting and decoration. The building itself looks solid and not unattractive, with a pleasant facade onto the street. This discovery surprised archaeologists, used to gloomy descriptions in Roman literature. Either Rome differed considerably from Ostia, or writers did not tell the whole story. For *insulae* at Ostia certainly did not only house the poor; there were stylish, elegant flats, for which high rents could reasonably be charged. But we should not overstate the comfort. There were no proper heating-systems, and no individual water-supplies. Although the outside of the block was brick and concrete, wooden furniture and open braziers made fire a constant threat. Ostia's records mention a fire which destroyed many *insulae*, on January 1st, AD 115. The lower floors were often more solidly built than higher storeys. Rooms at the top tended to be smaller, darker and flimsier.

These Ostian *insulae* provide most of our direct evidence. At Pompeii and Herculaneum a few *insulae* were built towards the time of the eruption, but here, away from over-populated Rome, most citizens had private houses.

The domus

BASIC PLAN

Pompeii and Herculaneum show the *domus* to its best advantage – one modern writer has called these homes:

The most wonderful of all the monuments that the ancient world has left . . . refuges of coolness, the realization of a Mediterranean ideal in a hot and noisy environment.   [M. Grant, *Cities of Vesuvius* p.3]

The main room was the *atrium* (hall), approached via the front door and porch. In its centre a rectangular pool (*impluvium*) stood beneath an opening in the roof (*compluvium*), the main source of light for the

15

The peristylium *of the House of the Vettii*

atrium; this let rain-water into the pool for domestic use. Slaves washed the dusty feet of guests in the *impluvium*, then the master and mistress received their guests in the *atrium*. Leading from this room were bedrooms and slaves' quarters; *tabernae* (small rooms) faced the street and were sometimes rented out as shops or lodgings.

From the *atrium*, the master's study (*tablinum*) usually led to the *peristylium*. This open courtyard was surrounded by a colonnade and rooms such as the dining-room (*triclinium*) and kitchen (*culina*). It was effectively the garden, since the houses faced inwards from the high outside walls which presented a blank mass onto the streets; there was no back or front garden. The House of the Vettii, where archaeologists have re-created a Roman garden, with flowers and fountains, shows why the *peristylium* was valued as a place for relaxation.

Not all houses had an identical pattern. Luxurious dwellings had two halls and two courtyards, and sometimes a private suite of baths and heating-system. For both of these the Romans used the *hypocaust*, an underfloor system, in which heat circulated between small pillars of bricks and rose in the cavities of walls.

INTERIOR DECORATION

Much interior decoration survives from these houses. Wall-paintings featured prominently, and because of special techniques, these have lasted extremely well. First the background was painted in on the prepared plaster. When this was dry, foreground figures were added. Finally a waxy glue gave a glossy finish, and acted as a preservative. Colours were obtained from minerals, or animal and vegetable dyes. Reds, oranges and blue-green dominated the pictures, but there were also yellows, black and purple. Popular subjects were mythological stories, country landscapes and still-life scenes with flowers, fruit and animals. Painters often used extremely realistic effects to deceive the viewer's eyes. In the 'architectural' style walls were painted with buildings, pillars and room-interiors; this often created an illusion of greater spaciousness, suggesting that the room continued beyond the wall – an effect nowadays achieved by using mirrors.

The 'fish mosaic' from the House of the Faun at Pompeii, composed in the style known as 'worm mosaic'

Mosaic-patterns and pictures were the standard floor-covering, and were sometimes used on walls or ceilings. The perfect preservation of some of these enables us to appreciate the styles and quality of craftsmanship. The earliest mosaics at Pompeii simply covered the floor with a plain geometric design of alternating black and white squares, but pictorial mosaics soon followed. The first mosaic-workers placed all the squares at the same angle. Later came the 'worm-mosaic' style, where artists arranged pieces of different shapes and sizes in series of curves. Sometimes the Pompeians imported complete mosaics from Greece, mounted on marble trays and ready to be slotted into place. Pattern-books enabled several copies of one design to be produced.

The rooms contained other artistic works such as bronze or marble statues. These were also placed in the *peristylium* as ornaments, producing a style of garden-decoration which has been frequently copied, and still is today.

FURNISHINGS

Evidence shows that by modern standards, houses were sparsely furnished. The bedrooms (small and functional) had practically nothing but the bed; the plain wooden bedframes, which have survived in a carbonised state, look rather uncomfortable, but there were mattresses and, for the rich, sumptuous quilts, to improve the appearance and comfort. In the *atrium* was the shrine for the household gods (*lararium*), and a sofa with mattresses and cushions.

Two cups from the 108-piece dinner-service found at the Boscoreale Villa

The *tablinum* had small and often expensive wooden or bronze chests and tables, and a safe-box for valuables. The dining-couches and tables in the *triclinium* were often the most luxurious items of furniture, with rare woods and silver or gold fittings. To our eyes, kitchens were cramped, stuffy and dangerous, with an open charcoal fire and assorted cooking-pots standing on metal grids. It was the slaves who did the cooking.

Thousands of smaller objects have been found. From Pompeii come bronze ladles, wine-jugs, dishes and bowls, glass bottles, gold, terracotta and bronze oil-lamps, a bronze heater giving a constant supply of hot water or wine, long, slender bronze candelabra, silver hand-mirrors, ivory and bone hairpins and combs, and gold jewellery of all kinds. There are even complete dinner-services, one with 108 pieces.

Not all homes possessed such refinements; furniture from *insulae* has long since disappeared. The poor rarely shared in the elegance of the *domus*.

3

Travel and the countryside

Roman writers tend to refer to Rome as *Urbs*, the City. In one sense, Rome *was* Roman Society, the seat of government and the commercial and artistic centre. But striking contrasts existed not only within the city, but between urban and rural life, between life in Italy and life in Greece, Britain or Egypt. So in this chapter we leave behind the city.

Travel by land

The Roman network of roads throughout the Empire is justly famous. Many survive, or have formed the basis for modern trunk-routes. Plutarch describes Roman road-construction as follows:

Roads were taken straight across the countryside without deviating; they were paved with hewn stones and supported with masses of tight-packed sand. The builders filled in hollows and built bridges over rivers or ravines which cut across the route. They kept the sides parallel and level. All in all, it presented a picture of smooth beauty.   [Plutarch, *Life of Gaius Gracchus* 7]

The poet Horace, describing a journey through Italy, mainly by road, presents a picture of the traveller's life:

I started from great Rome and stayed at Aricia . . . Then on to Appii Forum, crammed with innkeepers and nasty boatmen . . . Night was preparing to cloak the sky with shadow and light the stars in the sky when slaves started hurling insults at the boatmen, and vice-versa. 'Put in here.' 'You're cramming three hundred on board – whoa, that's enough!' A whole hour is wasted collecting fares and rounding up mules. You couldn't sleep – murderous mosquitoes, frogs in the swamps, and a sailor and passenger (drunk on stale wine) serenading their missing lady-loves . . . At dawn we noticed the boat wasn't moving, and some crackpot jumped up and started using a stick on the sailor and mule. Finally, about the fourth hour [10 a.m.] we docked.

This nautical interlude negotiated, they travelled on south, covering about thirty kilometres a day.

Then we made for Beneventum. The landlord was so keen to please that he almost burnt the place down while turning some scraggy thrushes on the fire. The flames got out of control and ran through the ancient kitchen towards the rooftops. The guests greedily grabbed up their dinner, and everyone started trying to put the fire out. [Horace, *Satires* I 5]

The rest of the journey was rather smoother – several thirty kilometre stages and then, with the end in sight, the final 120 kilometres covered in two days. Though not without incident, the safe completion of the journey owed much to the skill of Roman road-builders, and to the prolonged peace the Roman world enjoyed.

And by sea

Technical genius could not prevent the Mediterranean and Aegean Seas playing unforeseen tricks on sailors, and writers constantly mention the hazards of sea-travel. Many cargo-ships, in which passengers travelled, finished up on the ocean-bed, and now provide a rich quarry for marine archaeologists. Desperate prayers to Neptune preceded the voyage, and survivors made grateful thanks-offerings to him. The sailing-season limited sea-travel considerably. Between October and March few set sail because winter storms and heavy cloud-cover made navigation by the stars more difficult. Even in the season certain days were avoided for superstitious reasons. It was also unlucky to travel if you sneezed while going on board, or saw crows in the rigging or wreckage on the shore.

Journeys were under sail, with a large linen mainsail and small

A merchant-ship being loaded with corn

squaresail for manoeuvring. With a following wind it took as little as ten days (at six knots) from Rome to Alexandria, compared with at least two months by land. Ships ranged from small coastal vessels to the large merchantmen which plied the vast corn trade, especially from Alexandria. The *Isis* was one of these:

What a size she was! Fifty-five metres long, the ship's carpenter told me, and fifteen metres wide, with a hold fourteen metres deep. The mast – what a height, and the yard-arm and forestay! And how the stern rose, gradually curving until it ended in a goose's head, while at the other end was the flatter sweep of the prow, with figures of Isis on each side. Everything was incredible . . . and the safety all depended on a little old man who moved the huge steering-oar with a tiller that was no more than a stick!

[Lucian, *The Ship* 5]

Safety also depended on the co-operation of wind and wave, a combination which struck fear into the hearts of normally courageous

The Bay of Naples, showing important Roman towns

Romans. But despite such fear, many travelled, for business or pleasure – and spread the Roman way of life all around the Mediterranean.

Holiday resorts

Sixteen kilometres west of Naples, near the popular Lake Lucrinus, was Baiae, the most fashionable Roman seaside resort. Along the curving coastline of the Bay of Naples spread luxury villas and less lavish boarding houses. Not much of these remains – modern villas have replaced those of the Romans. But Herculaneum's wall-paintings and literary references show their character. To own such a villa (*villa maritima*) was a real status symbol. Cicero owned eight in the area, and one of his contemporaries, Lucullus, had a particularly grand villa near Naples: he had a tunnel dug through the mountains to bring salt water to his private fishponds. Emperors also favoured the area. Augustus and Tiberius acquired the island Capri for private use, and Nero attempted to poison his mother at Bauli. Villas were built along the coast, some right out into the sea, or on the hillside overlooking it. A long colonnade faced the sea, behind which were several rooms, all with good views. Larger villas had several colonnades rising above each other – anticipating the rooms with sea-views and balconies of modern hotels.

Wealthy senators sometimes owned a private fishpond – to breed rare fish for the table. Cicero called them the 'fishpond set', these senators who made for the coast at the Senate's spring break and spent their time inviting each other to banquets, doing their best to keep up with the Luculluses.

SEASIDE PLEASURES

Sea-bathing was never a great attraction. The popular places, such as Stabiae, for taking the waters were the hot springs, which were natural spas with healthy sulphur from the nearby volcanoes. Sightseeing in litters (sedan-chairs) or small pleasure-boats on the sea or lake was popular, and there were gastronomic attractions even for those without their own fishpond – Lake Lucrinus contained excellent shell-fish. Intellectuals liked the area, for its literary and philosophical discussions, concerts and plays. As today, seaside traders cashed in. Products ranged from luxury clothes to cheapjack souvenirs, including glass ornaments with rough drawings of local sights, labelled: 'Palace', 'Theatre', 'Nero's Pool', 'Oyster-beds'.

Above all, a holiday by the sea enabled people to let their hair down, including the inevitable holiday romance:

The wife was stricter than her stern husband:
A model of virtue.
One day she went to Lake Lucrinus,
Heated up in Baiae's baths.
The fire was in her –
She dropped her husband:
Ran off with a young gigolo.   [Martial, I 62]

A stern-minded contemporary of Cicero wrote of Baiae:

Unmarried girls are common property; old men act like teenagers, teenage boys like girls.   [Varro, *Satires* fr. 44]

Centuries later, a Roman aristocrat commented:

I always behave like a self-respecting consul. Even on Lake Lucrinus I preserve my dignity – no gadding about on yachts, gourmet banquets, visiting the baths – and none of the young set's nude mixed bathing-parties.
                                    [Symmachus, *Letters* 8 23 3]

Local industry

Through spring and summer tourists filled the towns, bringing commercial prosperity to local inhabitants – though the rich left the seaside when the hottest weather arrived, making for villas in the cooler hills: they would not have understood today's passion for sunbathing. But not all residents relied on the seasonal income of the tourist trade. Some towns, including Pompeii, depended also on local produce and foreign trade. The Campanian plain, with its fertile volcanic soil, yielded corn, vines and olives. Pompeian wine was famous, not least for causing hang-overs. The town manufactured storage-jars (*amphorae*) for wine, olive-oil and Pompeii's other famous product – *garum*. This fish-sauce was created by a complicated process. Entrails of sprats and sardines were mixed with finely chopped portions of fish and fish-eggs, then pounded, crushed and stirred together. The mixture was left in a warm place to ferment and evaporate, then placed in a basket with holes in the base for the *garum* to filter through to another container. Pompeian *garum* was exported all over the Empire. Another important industry, the cloth-trade, used wool from nearby highland sheep.

VILLAE RUSTICAE

Houses in Pompeii were often workshops or small factories for the agriculturally-based industries, as were villas outside the town, such as that at Boscoreale. This was a *villa rustica*, the working centre of an agricultural estate and essentially different from the *villae maritimae* or, inland, *villae urbanae* – devoted largely to their owners' pleasure. Although often owned by wealthy landlords, *villae rusticae* were worked by slave labour and supervised by the *vilicus* (bailiff). There were also smaller estates owned by farmers of moderate means, or rented by tenant-farmers.

The plan of the Boscoreale villa shows how such estates operated. Notice that corn, olives and wine all featured prominently. There were granaries, an oil-press and wine-producing establishment with wine-press, large storage-jars, tanks for the dregs, and a large cellar to store the *amphorae*, buried with their necks just above floor-level.

Town-dwellers today often forget the closeness of the link between town and country – they buy food in forms far removed from the original farm product; peas frozen solid in plastic bags, not crunchy and juicy in their pods. But the Romans were always in touch with their agricultural roots. Even city-dwellers longed for the countryside.

THE FARMER'S LIFE

Villae rusticae provide valuable evidence of Roman farming, and so do the modern techniques of aerial photography, with their graphic illustrations of land-use. There are also Roman writers such as Virgil, himself a countryman. His *Georgics* describe many aspects of agricultural life, and pay tribute to the farmer's work:

The farmer tills the earth with curved plough.
This is his annual toil; from this he supports
Land and family, herds of cattle and fine oxen . . .
The cows offer milk-filled udders, and plump kids
On the joyful plain test each other with locked horns . . .
Such a life the Sabines of old once kept.
Thus lived Romulus and Remus; thus grew brave Etruria
And Rome became the prince of nations.
[Virgil, *Georgics* II 513–5 524–6 532–4]

Virgil thought the farmer's life had lessons for mankind. For example, bee-keeping:

25

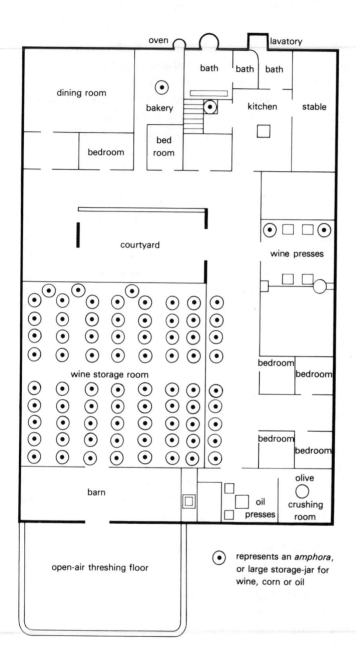

A plan of the Villa Boscoreale, with bakery and oil and wine-making equipment

26

Bees alone share their children in common.
They live in a city, united beneath one roof,
And pass their lives under ordered laws.
They know their native country, their hearth and home.
Aware of winter's approach, they toil hard in summer
Placing the fruits of labour in a common pool . . .
All is a seething mass of industry.
The fragrant honey is perfumed with thyme.

[Virgil, *Georgics* IV 153–7 169]

FARMING METHODS

Leaving aside such flights of fancy, the farmer's life was no bed of roses. Farm implements meant solid, manual labour: spades and shovels, mattocks, hoes and axes, knives, sickles, hooks and scythes, forks, saws, shears. Mechanical assistance came only from ploughs and, on some larger farms, reaping-machines and threshing-machines like that described below:

The grain should be threshed on the floor. In some districts this is done by a yoke of oxen and a threshing-sledge (*tribulum*). The machine is constructed of a board, roughened with stones or pieces of iron fixed in it, which separates the grain from the ear of corn when the oxen drag it along, if there is a driver or heavy object in the sledge.   [Varro, *Country Life* I 52 2]

The farmer's life centred on the plough, pulled by a pair of oxen. Ploughing occupied a substantial part of the year; often farmers ploughed three or four times to ensure a good 'tilth', to make the most of their land. Fields were largely devoted to corn; the Romans grew wheat and barley. But despite the farmers' best efforts, Imperial Rome needed huge imports of grain.

To improve efficiency, farmers experimented with crop-rotation and the design of their equipment. But it was still hard, unglamorous work. Virgil's picture of the peasant farmer, the backbone of early Rome, certainly had a foundation in fact. Early in Rome's history, the farmer Cincinnatus was said to have been appointed dictator in a military crisis. He defeated the enemy and returned immediately to his ploughing. In those early days, citizens farmed the land, and there were fewer slaves. But Rome's wars and conquests throughout the Mediterranean had a drastic effect. Many left their farms to fight and never returned. Others found their land swallowed up by large estates (*latifundia*), and never recovered it. The influx of slaves brought cheaper labour to the land-owners, and the number of citizen-farmers

27

A reconstruction of Pliny's Laurentine villa

rapidly contracted. The landlords often only dabbled in farming. For them, land was fundamentally an investment, though they shared the Roman craving for country life. But while they indulged their romantic ideas, slaves in chain-gangs bent low, working long hours in the fields under the fierce heat of the sun, spurred on by the whip. For them, the prospect of the countryside was the worst possible punishment.

Dreams of the country

The rural dream was more often based on the *villa urbana* than the *villa rustica*, as Pliny the Younger shows:

> You seem surprised that I am so keen on my Laurentine villa. You'll understand if I tell you how delightful the house itself is, what an excellent situation it has, and what a wide view of the sea . . . There are varied attractions on both sides as you approach. First the road narrows and passes through a wood, then it widens and goes through rolling fields. Flocks of sheep, herds of cattle and horses, driven by winter's cold down from the hills, graze happily on the grass there; the climate is springlike.
>
> [Pliny the Younger, *Letters* II 17]

For Pliny, rolling fields and sheep and cattle are mere pastoral adornments to his ideal existence – a peaceful country retreat in pleasant surroundings, away from the anxieties of city life. Even Juvenal, whose *Satires* hum with the pace of the city, imagines a friend inviting him to leave Rome:

Who ever feared his home would collapse in cool Praeneste, or Volsinii up among the wooded hillsides, or simple Gabii, or Tivoli, perched on the brow of the hill? But here, the city we inhabit is largely shored up by thin wooden props . . . Tear yourself away from the Circuses. There's a fine home waiting for you at Sora, Fabrateria or Frusino. A year's rent for your dark garret here will buy it. A garden, a shallow well (no need for rope and bucket when you're watering the young vines). Live to love the hoe. Look after an allotment producing enough to feed a hundred vegetarians. Whatever remote corner you're in, you'll be lord and master of the local lizard – that's something! . . . But it's sunset, and the cattle are lowing. I must go. The mule man's been beckoning me for some time. Goodbye; remember me. Whenever Rome releases you to go to your native Aquinum, invite me over . . . I'll share the country with you, and the rustic festivals. And if you don't despise my help, I'll come over in my best country galoshes and help you write satires.

[Juvenal, *Satires* III *passim*]

4
Social divisions

Citizenship

Vast inequalities within Roman society should not surprise us, since even countries where equality is a declared ideal have not given everyone equal wealth or status. At Rome, the differences were reflected in the rigid class-structure which affected all citizens, but still more fundamental was the distinction between those who possessed citizenship and those who did not.

Three groups of men qualified for citizenship:

1 Those whose parents were Roman citizens (the 'free-born').
2 Those freed from slavery (freedmen).
3 Those granted citizenship by the government, either individuals or communities within the Roman Empire.

All citizens shared basic privileges, the most important being protection under Roman law. Wherever they were, they could apply for a legal hearing at Rome. They could also marry into citizen families, and qualify for State benefits such as free corn, tickets for the public shows, and use of the suites of baths.

The expansion of the Empire altered the citizen population. Rome, as capital of the Empire, attracted many immigrants from different countries. Immigration was not always popular. Juvenal wrote contemptuously: 'The Orontes (a Syrian river) has flowed into the Tiber', as though Rome was being polluted by foreign influences. But immigration could not be stopped, and gradually more and more people at Rome and throughout the Empire obtained citizenship. In time there were even emperors born outside Italy: first from Spain, then Africa, then the East.

THE SENATORIAL CLASS

The highest group of citizens was the senatorial class, where the head of the family (*paterfamilias*) was a senator. The Senate was Rome's nearest equivalent to a parliament, composed of 600 to 900 of the wealthiest citizens. It was the governing body during the Republic, but under the emperors had a subordinate role, though it continued to influence decisions. Senators received no salary; their continuing wealth depended largely on profits from land-ownership. They had to own property worth over one million sesterces, and once a family achieved a place in the Senate, it largely retained the status; barring financial or political disaster, the senator stayed a senator for life, trying to work through the *cursus honorum* (ladder of offices): *quaestor, aedile* or *tribune, praetor* and finally *consul*. There were therefore grades of importance within the Senate, and junior senators, who had to wait their turn, rarely participated in debates.

THE EQUESTRIAN ORDER

Below senators came the *equites* (often known as the 'equestrian order'). Originally *equites* (literally 'knights') had the privilege of riding a horse on public ceremonial occasions, but this tradition was largely forgotten as *equites* became simply wealthy citizens outside the Senate who possessed the necessary property qualification of 400,000 sesterces. Although most took no part in politics, emperors used them increasingly as a 'civil service': some advised the emperor personally; some held important administrative positions in the Empire. Many were Italian landowners; others grew rich (often amassing large fortunes) through trade or financial dealings – particularly the collection of taxes in provinces like Asia.

LOWER CITIZEN-CLASSES

The bulk of citizens were neither senators nor *equites*. These were divided into five classes with decreasing property qualifications. All other citizens were known as *capite censi* (literally 'counted by head') because they did not qualify for any of these five classes.

SLAVES AND FREEDMEN

Citizens were distinguished from free-born non-citizen members of other communities within the Empire, and also from slaves.[1] Slaves could buy their freedom if their masters agreed, by using the small sum of money (*peculium*) they received for work. Alternatively, they could

[1] For an account of the conditions and work of slaves, see *Roman Slavery* in this series, by M. Massey and P. Moreland.

be freed in their master's will or for loyal service. A Roman-owned slave, once he was a freedman (*libertus*), could become a citizen – although with restricted rights. His former master now became his patron (*patronus*), and the freedman, now his client (*cliens*), adopted two of his patron's three names, in addition to his single slave-name. Some freedmen then entered business on their own behalf and prospered though few approached the amazing wealth of Pallas, a personal secretary of the Emperor Claudius:

Pallas was awarded an honorary praetorship, and the elected consul, Soranus, proposed the reward of fifteen million sesterces . . . Claudius reported that Pallas would only accept the honour, he preferred to rest content with his present modest fortune. Thereupon the Senate engraved the decree in bronze letters, praising Pallas warmly for his fine example of traditional frugality – this for a man once a slave and now worth three million sesterces.

[Tacitus, *Annals* XII 53]

Patrons and clients

Patronage was an idea that ran through the whole of Roman society. It is a system which operates when the client needs money or influence from some person or company (the patron, or sponsor), and the patron can see some return for the 'favour', such as political support, or prestige and the spread of one's name.

In Rome, everyone except the emperor was someone's client. Consequently, someone could be both client and patron simultaneously. A wealthy freedman, for instance, had many poor clients, but remained the client of his own patron. The poet Martial, who often gives us the client's viewpoint, resented this two-way system:

I'm angling for dinner with you, Maximus –
I'm ashamed to admit it, but I am.
You're after another man's dinner –
So that makes us equals.
I come to greet you in the morning,
But they tell me
You've already gone to greet another.
I'm your personal attendant,
Walking before my haughty lord.
You escort another man –
So now we're equals.
It's enough to be a slave,

Without being a slave's slave.
A lord, Maximus,
Shouldn't have a lord himself.   [Martial, II 18]

POLITICAL PATRONAGE

Patronage could help a political career. During the Republic, the
aspiring senator needed his client's votes at elections: without 'mass
media', the most successful politician was often the one most frequently seen and heard. Candidates therefore wanted crowds of clients to
appear at the *salutatio* (greeting them at home in the morning) and the
deductio (escorting them to the Forum). These everyday events for the
wealthy patron acquired special significance at election-time.

By transferring elections from the people's assembly to the Senate,
the emperors took away the need to worry about clients' votes.
However, political patronage was still necessary. Ambitious politicians now needed the backing of influential senators, and if possible
the emperor:

My friend Sextus Erucius is standing for office, a matter which concerns me
greatly – I actually feel more nervous about him than I ever did for myself.
Besides, my own honour, reputation and position are all caught up in this,
since I persuaded the Emperor to promote Sextus to the senatorial class as
quaestor; and now, with my support, he is standing for *tribune* . . . I am
therefore approaching all my friends, begging their support . . . You are such
a popular man, much admired and in great demand, and once you show your
backing, many others will want to be on your side.
                              [Pliny the Younger, *Letters* II 9]

THE DOLE

Most clients' ambitions were less exalted than this. It was a question of
survival, in a world without an elaborate range of social security
benefits. Many who were unemployed could not even buy basic food
requirements without State intervention. Under the emperors, this aid
was increasingly linked with the wealthy. They gave a regular 'dole'
(*sportula*) of food or money, or an invitation to dinner, to poor clients.
These could generally do little about ungenerous patrons, except seek
someone new. But Martial at least got his own back in his poems:

I have to climb the high track uphill from the Subura,
The dirty pavement with steps always wet.
I can hardly get through the long mule-trains

And blocks of marble hauled along by ropes.
Then, after my exertions, there's still worse:
When I arrive, tired out, your doorman tells me
You're not at home: my reward for useless toil and soaking toga.

[Martial, V 22]

Martial tells us that in his days the fixed rate for the dole was six and a
quarter sesterces – not very much, but for the unemployed (out of
work schoolmasters, lawyers, poets or artists, as well as the unskilled)
all they had. Even on this paltry allowance, clients were expected to
arrive wearing a toga, proving their citizenship. Martial didn't think
much of this:

For three *denarii* [twice the normal dole], Bassus, you invite me
To your *atrium* in the morning wearing a toga;
Then to stay by your side, walk before your litter
And call on about ten widows with you.
I know my toga's cheap, old and worn,
But I can't buy a new one for three *denarii*, Bassus.   [Martial, IX 100]

The white woollen toga (symbol of citizenship) was wrapped elabo-
rately around the body over the *tunica* (tunic). It was an expensive

A Roman wearing the toga (symbol of citizenship)

item. Some patrons gave clients a new toga on special occasions as a present, to ensure their smart appearance, which reflected well on themselves. So, properly dressed, the clients waited in strict order of class to see their patron. Once admitted, respectful address was important:

Caecilianus, this morning I addressed you by name,
But forgot to add 'My lord';
A careless slip, which cost me dearly:
I lost my daily bread. [Martial, VI 88]

Another description comes from the pen of Juvenal:

In the old days, clients were guests. Now Roman citizens in togas wait in crowds and scramble on their patron's doorway for their tiny allowance. The great man stares closely at each face, making sure no cheats turn up under false pretences. You only get your rations when you've passed this scrutiny.

Nor was the *salutatio* the end of it:

So the day wears on with its set routine, that round of duties – *so* fascinating. After pocketing his dole, he has to attend 'my lord' to the Forum and stare at the statues, bored stiff . . . Then follow the patron home, hoping desperately for a dinner-invitation which never comes. Finally the poor wretches wander off, utterly exhausted, to buy their cabbage and firewood.

[Juvenal, *Satires* I *passim*]

This existence was shared by many thousands.

Women

The attempt to obtain a full picture of women in Roman society is more difficult because so little that women themselves wrote has survived. One of the few remaining fragments comes from a woman who wrote poems of her love for a certain Cerinthus. Her name was Sulpicia:

I hate my birthday but it's coming soon.
I hate the country too –
But I'll have to go there,
Sad as it makes me.
And without Cerinthus!
What could be nicer than staying in town?
Is a farmhouse a fit place for a girl?
[fragments from the poems of Sulpicia (Tib. III xiv=IV viii, 1–3)]

Apart from such brief personal statements, the picture must be made up from male accounts, and a variety of types of archaeological evidence.

ATTITUDES TO MARRIAGE

To a degree, the position of women in Roman society always depended on prevailing attitudes to marriage. The freer these were, the freer women tended to be. Romans at first saw marriage as a woman's passing from her father's control into her husband's, so a Roman woman was definitely regarded as the submissive partner – without man's legal rights, as an old law shows:

If anyone catches his wife with another man, he can have her put to death without trial . . . But if the man commits adultery, the wife can do nothing: she has no legal rights against her husband.

[Aulus Gellius, *Attic Nights* 10 23 5]

Times changed attitudes. Laws about adultery became less severe, and divorce became common, with either the woman or the man free to break the contract.

Many Romans married for financial or social reasons. Since the bride was accompanied by a dowry, marriage into a noble family could be a means of achieving wealth and social status. The connection between 'love and marriage' did not necessarily apply: many marriages were for convenience – for example, to strengthen a political alliance. Several emperors contracted such marriages. Tiberius was forced to divorce Vipsania, whom he loved, to marry Augustus' daughter Julia, whom he could not stand.

But within such a limited concept of marriage, many were happily married, as inscriptions and literature record.

Pliny the Younger married a girl much younger than him, about fifteen. He expressed his delight with her in writing to her aunt:

Calpurnia has proved worthy of her father, grandfather and yourself. She is intelligent and a careful housewife. Her devotion to me shows that she is a good girl; it has caused her to take interest in literature. She keeps copies of my works, to read over and over to herself, even learning some by heart . . . If I am giving a reading, she sits behind a curtain nearby and listens eagerly to every appreciative comment. She has even set my verses to music and sings them, accompanying herself on the lyre – despite having no music teacher except love, the best tutor. [Pliny the Younger, *Letters* IV 19]

It sounds loving and idyllic, but the relationship appears more like that between a distinguished professor and an admiring young student than a husband and wife on equal terms. Pliny approves of Calpurnia mainly because of her devotion to *him*. Perhaps the following extract gives more idea of a marriage where the husband respected his wife for herself:

We have been fortunate enough to have enjoyed a marriage lasting forty-one years, without difficulties. It is indeed rare for such long marriages to end in death rather than divorce. But I only wish I had been the one to die first. As I was older than you, this would have been much fairer.

I need not recall such everyday qualities as your goodness, obedience, kindness, upright character or skill at weaving . . . You share these with many other married women who wish to be well thought of. What I treasure most are those qualities which belong to you alone. These have enabled you to withstand terrible difficulties, and to perform services which few have ever equalled. . . .

The memory of your virtues and fine character will encourage and inspire me to resist fortune's blows . . . I will end by declaring that you deserved the very best, and I wish that I had been able to give you the very best . . . I pray that your guardian spirits may grant you peace and keep you at rest.

[*In Praise of Turia, passim*]

'MODERN WOMEN'

Some male literature gave women an extremely hostile press. Juvenal devoted a satire of over 600 lines to what he felt was wrong with the women of his day. He complained that they were no longer modest and unassuming, like the old-fashioned ideal wife, quietly staying at home and supervising the household and spinning:

If you're looking for a woman with decent old-fashioned moral standards, you must be out of your mind . . . you'd be hard pushed to find a girl who'd kept off sex for nine days!

Women even tried to imitate men, Juvenal says:

Worse still is the butch woman who runs around town barging in on stag-parties, being cheeky to uniformed generals in front of her embarrassed husband . . . Look at her, a fearful sight, setting off to the baths with her oil-jars and the rest of the gear. A work-out on the weights to generate a sweat then, exhausted, it's over to the skilled attentions of the masseur . . . Then off to the sauna, sitting there among the din while her guests wait at her house for dinner, absolutely starving.

Others were excessively devoted to beauty-treatments:

Take your fashionable woman, all decked out in emerald necklaces, and ears weighed down with enormous pearls. When she's preparing to venture forth she looks so awful it's hilarious. You can't see her face beneath the thick face-pack; she's covered in grease and cream – it sticks to your lips if you kiss her. Finally, when her features start to emerge from the layers, she smears them all over with asses' milk . . . You wonder what's underneath – a face or a nasty sore . . .

If she wants to look her best for a date, she rushes round like mad. She's late, and her lover is waiting for her in the park . . ., so she summons the slavegirl who does her hair. 'Why's this curl out of place?', she screams. (It's the whip for a curl out of place.) Is it the girl's fault you don't like the shape of your nose? Next stage of the operation: another girl on the left combs out the offending lock and twists it on the curlers. Then the 'Advisory Board' is joined by one of mother's old maidservants. The juniors have to wait for her decision. You'd think the mistress's good name or life was at stake, the fantastic trouble they go to. Finally it's complete. The tall edifice rises, storey on storey.

[Juvenal, *Satires* VI *passim*]

WOMEN AT LEISURE

Juvenal strikes his target with ruthless observation. The tilt about hairstyles is easily understood by looking at sculptures of the period. For a noblewoman to prepare herself for going out was an elaborate, time-consuming performance, which had to be undergone every day. But we can understand why such activities filled her day. Slaves looked after every domestic task, and a slave looked after the slaves. There was little left to do. Some women tried to escape from the role which society imposed on them. Gradually they gained more independence, and undertook new activities:

Ummidia Quadratilla is dead. She was almost seventy-nine and in excellent health until her final illness . . . She used to keep a band of actors, treating them rather too indulgently for a noblewoman . . . Once when she was entrusting her grandson's education to me, she told me that when (with all that spare time women have) she was intending to pass the hours playing draughts or watching the actors, she always sent him away to study.

[Pliny the Younger, *Letters* VII 24]

Pliny felt that games of draughts (and a rather too intimate relationship with actors) were not the proper thing for a noblewoman, and were unsuitable for her grandson to watch. But even he admits that women had long hours with nothing to do, and this must be borne in mind

A Roman noblewoman with an elevated hairstyle

when judging writers' severe comments about women's behaviour. The poet Ovid, who encouraged women to enjoy themselves, forgetting the traditional way of life, horrified some male contemporaries. Among these was Augustus who, at the time, was trying to revive the old ways. He exiled Ovid partly because of comments such as these in his poetry:

Others can praise the good old days; I'm only glad I'm a modern man; this is the time for me! . . .
We men are attracted by neat elegance. Don't let your hair be unruly – hands carefully applied create beauty.
There's no one right hairstyle; decide, in front of a mirror, the style which suits you best . . .
One girl's hair should be let down over her shoulders, another's fastened back; one is suited by hair blowing freely in the wind, another should keep her hair tightly-plaited.
But there are no golden rules – and every day there's some new fashion.

[Ovid, *The Art of Love* III *passim*]

Ovid was advising women how to attract men, and he shows an awareness of 'female psychology' which makes a change from the heavy male attitudes which dominate Latin literature. Yet even *his* writing is really aiming to make women fit in with men's desires.

39

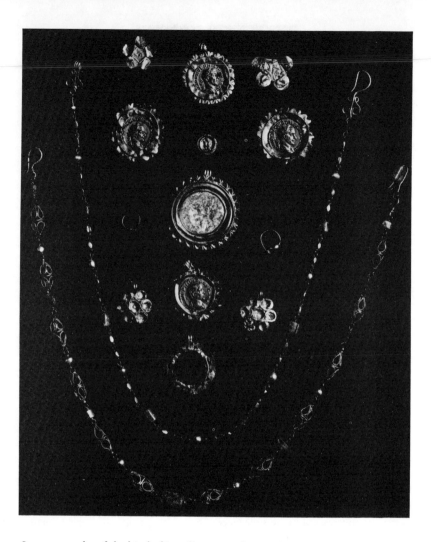

Some examples of the kind of jewellery worn by wealthy Roman women

OTHER EVIDENCE

We rely on archaeology for examples of women's toiletries, jewellery and clothing-styles, and on scattered references in tomb inscriptions and graffiti. Epitaphs show that the increasing independence of noblewomen had parallels lower in the social scale. Women undertook men's work, becoming wool-sellers, secretaries (normally a male occupation), even doctors and teachers. The walls of Pompeii give glimpses of other women:

Vibius Restitutus slept here alone, homesick and missing his Urbana.

[*CIL* iv 2146]

The nice barmaid is thirsty. I'm asking you.
Calpurnia is thirsty. She's telling you.   [*CIL* iv 1819]
The little blonde told me to steer clear of brunettes.
I will if I can. If not, I'll love them despite myself.

And a sad note:

Noete, light of my life, goodbye, goodbye, forever goodbye.

5

Varieties of work

Education and work

The word 'work' makes many students think immediately of school, no doubt with mixed feelings. School certainly is a kind of work; it is also a preparation for adult work. How far was this true of Roman education, and what were the Romans' attitudes towards education? We shall be dealing with these questions here.[1]

PRIMARY EDUCATION

Rome provided no free state education, but primary education was relatively cheap, and taught children what they might need for many adult occupations – reading, writing and arithmetic, and little else. Many parents thought it worth securing this education for their sons, and often for their daughters. Pupils were at primary school for five to six years, from about six years old. With so much time to learn so few skills, teaching methods could afford to be slow. The teacher, *ludi magister* (schoolmaster) or *litterator* (teacher of letters), generally taught a small class in an open space or small rented apartment (*taberna*) in a private house. Upper-class children arrived accompanied by a Greek slave, *paedagogus*, who stayed with them all day. He also helped the children learn Greek, and many grew up bi-lingual in Latin and Greek.

They wrote on slates (the surface coated with dark wax for writing to show up), using a *stilus* – a sharp-pointed pen of metal, wood, bone or ivory, with a flat end to rub out finished work. The teacher would write a fair copy which the children then copied and so practised their writing skills. Such copying-exercises often contained good advice:

Work hard, boy, or you'll be thrashed.

---

[1]For a fuller account, see *Greek and Roman Education* (R. Barrow), in this series.

A piece of schoolboy writing from Rome shows a heavily-laden donkey with the comment:

Work hard, ass, as I've had to – and much good will it do you!

Pupils learned to identify and pronounce each letter separately and in combinations, long before meeting actual words. This lengthy process, aimed at thorough knowledge, suited a phonetically-written language like Latin, but it was hardly exciting. Occasionally teachers introduced variety, devising tongue-twisters with the letters of the alphabet in different orders; one made his class little cakes in the shape of the letters; another had a procession of slaves carrying placards on their backs, each showing a different letter.

Larger schools had an arithmetic assistant, the *calculator*. (By a strange irony, the word now signifies not an 'arithmetic-teacher' but an 'arithmetic-substitute'.) Pupils learned to count by a system where different hand-positions stood for the numbers, and by using the abacus – a frame with beads or pebbles, which could work out complicated calculations, including fractions. The abacus is still in use today, for example in Russia.

The poet Horace objected to arithmetic teachers because they made children reject the arts for materialistic concerns:

Is it any wonder when children are taught this love of money that they are not interested in becoming poets?   [Horace, *The Art of Poetry* 330–1]

This reflects perhaps the oldest debate about education: should people receive education for its own sake or its future value?

SECONDARY EDUCATION

After leaving the *litterator*, children were equipped for basic commercial transactions. Boys might now become apprenticed to such trades as carpentry; most girls stayed at home until marriage.

The teacher at the second stage was the *grammaticus*. Like the *litterator*, he was often Greek, and was usually poorly paid. Writers often mention the poverty of schoolmasters, though there were a few exceptions such as the *grammaticus* Epaphroditus, who taught at Rome in the time of Nero, and died owning two houses in Rome and a celebrated library. His portrait is the only surviving picture identifiable as a Roman schoolmaster.

Those who stayed on were mainly the sons of the rich, but some

Epaphroditus   *Cicero*

ambitious parents wanted their children to better themselves through education. Horace's father was one:

If I have lived a decent life, I owe it to my father. Though he was poor . . . he sent me to Rome, to learn the things a senator's son learned.

[Horace, *Satires* I 6 68–71 and 76–8]

And what were these? Juvenal puts it in a nutshell:

Eloquence, that's what they're after, the whole lot. Even the schoolboy . . . spends all his time praying that one day he'll become as good and successful a speaker as Cicero.   [Juvenal, *Satires* X 114–117]

The ability to use words was certainly the fundamental skill. The programme, taught largely to twelve – sixteen year-old boys, consisted basically of literature, especially poetry. Pupils studied Latin and Greek poems, recited long sections of them and learned to deliver lines accurately and stylishly. There was also elementary training in rhetoric, the art of making speeches, and informal instruction in history, geography and astronomy (largely to explain references in poems). As Horace owed his success to poetry, he had every reason to feel grateful to his father.

44

Although not everyone could or would spend money to educate children like this, knowledge of poetry was evidently widespread. All over the walls of Pompeii are lines from Roman poets. The scribblers could not always spell properly the lines they had learned by heart, but something of their education had stuck. Roman writers raised few objections to this narrow secondary education, but the philosopher Seneca disapproved:

> Literary studies are concerned with language, history and poetry . . . But which of these can put a man on the road to virtue? . . . How can they help us remove fear, or control passions and desires?
>
> [Seneca, *Letters to Lucilius* LXXXVII *passim*]

Seneca was really demanding 'moral education', as it is now known, but this was not something most Romans took seriously, at least for secondary education. They accepted the education of the *grammaticus* as a preparation for the third stage.

RHETOR AND RHETORIC

The *rhetor* taught wealthy boys from the age of about sixteen; as his name suggests, he gave instruction mainly in rhetoric, public speaking. This course did have a practical, vocational aim for some. Sons of Roman senators largely considered two careers (often combined): politics and law, for which public speaking was essential. These courses may have contributed to a rapid rise in the numbers of lawyers at Rome. Republican politicians like Cicero often made their name in the law-courts. In the Empire, senators did not rely on popular appeal, but they still felt the need to speak well. There developed great interest in delivering speeches as a form of entertainment. Just as poets drew crowds to hear poetry-recitals, speech-makers filled lecture-halls; audiences heard them holding forth on any subject under the sun, a skill they acquired from the *rhetor*, as Juvenal shows:

> Are you a *rhetor*? You must be a tough man with a thick skin if you can sit through the whole class's performance of 'Down with the Tyrant'. They learn it by heart, and recite it out loud, all trotting out the same tired phrases and clichés, the same boring diet for the teacher a thousand times.
>
> [Juvenal, *Satires* VII 150–4]

Teachers may have found such set speeches wearisome, but it was probably worse for the students, drilled endlessly in repetitious exercises. It was an elaborate process. Students learned the theory of rhetoric, studying examples from Greek and Latin literature. They did practical exercises, composing suitable speeches for weddings and funerals. Then there were formal set speeches – *controversiae*, where students argued cases in imaginary lawsuits, and *suasoriae*, where the speeches were on non-legal cases, such as 'Down with the Tyrant'.

This stage of education gave many the start in life they needed for a prosperous existence as senator and barrister. They might finish their training by a spell at places such as Athens to study philosophy or Rhodes for further rhetorical training; here there were institutions comparable to universities. Then they often spent a short time in the army as junior officers, widening their experience and perhaps preparing for a future position as provincial governor.

Various occupations

UPPER-CLASS ROMANS AT WORK

One Roman who followed this process was Pliny the Elder, uncle and guardian of the younger Pliny, who describes his daily routine. He catalogues his 104 volumes, which he had completed when he died aged fifty-five, and continues:

From the middle of August he started to work by lamplight, simply to give himself more time for study, and he rose in the middle of the night. In winter this was often at midnight or an hour later – two at the latest . . . Before dawn he visited the Emperor Vespasian, who also worked at night, and then attended to official duties. Back home he spent any spare time working, then had something to eat . . . In summer (if he was not too busy) he often lay in the sun while a book was read to him, making notes and taking down passages. He did this with every book he read, for he said that no book was so bad that there was nothing useful in it. After this he usually had a cold bath, another snack and a siesta, then worked till dinner just as though he had begun a new day. Even during the meal a book was read aloud, and he made notes in shorthand . . .

When he travelled, he felt free from other commitments to concentrate on his work, so his secretary stayed beside him with book and jotting tablets; in winter he protected his hands with long sleeves – he wouldn't let the cold weather rob him of an hour's work. This is why he was carried about in a litter when in Rome. He always told me off for walking. In his view, I needn't have wasted this time. (Any time not spent working was wasted, according to him.) This was the kind of dedication it took to finish so many books.

[Pliny the Younger, *Letters* III 5 *passim*]

Evidently, wealthy Romans could live extremely busy lives. Often not only work but an endless round of social obligations (as patrons) occupied their time. Senatorial duties (committees, reports, speeches) could be a time-consuming business for the conscientious, though few, if any, quite shared Pliny's relentless work-output.

BUSINESSMEN

The senatorial class was legally barred from any form of commercial or trading business. Commercial life was dominated by the *equites*, who ran businesses, collected taxes, became bankers or money-lenders, and controlled trading-companies as shippers. Skilled freedmen also participated in these activities. The outstanding example is a character from fiction, Trimalchio. In a novel by Petronius, Trimalchio describes his rise to riches:

As I was saying, it was my quick way with money that got me to my present position. I arrived from Asia no higher than this candlestick . . . gradually, I took charge in the house. I was the old man's favourite – he thought of nobody but me. Finally he made me joint heir with the emperor: result – a cool million from his will, enough to make me a senator if I'd wanted. But the sky's the limit, so I wanted to start in business. I built five ships, filled them with wine (gold-dust at that time) and sent them to Rome. But would you believe it? Every single ship destroyed in a shipwreck – straight gospel! Neptune got his teeth into thirty million that day. But did I give up? Not likely! I built more ships . . . loaded them up again – wine, bacon, beans, slaves, perfume. Then my dearly beloved Fortunata stumped up – sold off her gold bits and bobs and clothes, and put ten thousand gold pieces in my hand. That was just what I needed – your luck's bound to change sooner or later. One voyage, and I was ten million better off. So I bought up my former master's estates, built a house, invested in slaves – everything I touched turned to gold. Once I'd got more than the rest of the country put together, I stopped – retired from business and started to live off the interest.   [Petronius, *Satyricon* 75–76]

Trimalchio was certainly based on living examples of men who went from rags to riches.

Other kinds of work

The range of occupations among Rome's 'lower' classes was vast. Some were considered more respectable than others:

We should reject as unsuitable those occupations which make others dislike us, such as being a tax-collector or money-lender. Also, we should not wish to become hired workmen, paid wages for unskilled manual labour. Such payments virtually make them slaves. As for retailers, selling produce which they bought wholesale, they could not make profits unless they sometimes traded dishonestly – the lowest kind of activity. Then consider the factories where those doing mechanical tasks work – they can't be at all civilized. The lowest occupations of all are those which cater for the pleasures of the senses – 'fishmonger, butcher, cook, poulterer and fisherman' (as the playwright Terence puts it), and we could add actors and dancers.

[Cicero, *On Moral Duties* I 42]

Cicero and his class disapproved strongly of citizens receiving wages, and hired workmen always had low status. Some tasks Cicero disliked were often done by slaves, along with work like mining, which citizens never undertook. But all these jobs had to be done.

Even today, not all shops are supermarkets or hypermarkets, selling everything from cauliflowers to coffee-grinders. At Rome, traders usually specialised in a single product. Larger groups were organised into 'guilds', which often had great influence. At Pompeii the most powerful was the guild of fullers, who laundered and prepared togas and other woollen articles. They had a large guildhall in the town forum, and featured prominently in local elections, as inscriptions show:

L. CEIVM SECVNDVM IIVIRVM IVRE DICVNDO PRIMVS FVLLO ROGAT
The fuller Primus asks for support for Lucius Ceius Secundus as duumvir.

[*CIL* iv 3478]

HOLCONIVM PRISCVM IIVIRVM FVLLONES VNIVERSI ROGANT
The united fullers support Holconius for duumvir.   [*CIL* iv 7164]

Tombstones mention over 150 guilds, including fruitsellers, melon-sellers, greengrocers, fishermen, wine-merchants, tavern-keepers, bakers, millers, pastry-cooks, confectioners, perfumers, florists, ring-sellers, ivory-sellers, goldsmiths, jewellers, dressmakers, shoemakers, dyers, embroiderers, silk-merchants, tanners, furriers, ropemakers, ironworkers, masons, timber-workers, muledrivers, oarsmen, porters, dockers.

For many of these, there is no record of their working-conditions, but we have detailed evidence about others, sometimes from mosaics or wall-paintings. Such illustrations show fullers at work – treading cloth in tubs (with water and alkaline agents), beating it with mallets, brushing it with teasel-burrs to raise the nap, bleaching it with sulphur and rubbing it with dry white earth before pressing it ready for sale. Also, shops may provide evidence. Twenty bakers'-shops have been excavated in Pompeii, one with a mill still in working order – large

48

Remains of a bakery at Pompeii. On the left is an oven and on the right a row of mills where corn was ground to make flour

mills were worked by donkeys turning the huge millstones. Even Pompeian bread, carbonised, has survived – a round, flat loaf cut into eight wedges, with the baker's name stamped on it. From such evidence information can be obtained about some of the humbler workers in Roman Society.

The city poor

Concentrated in Rome were also many with no regular employment. Many, like the dispossessed farmers driven from their land by the large slave-manned *latifundia*, had little hope of a fresh start as traders or craftsmen, since they lacked capital, skill and experience. Their presence caused great social problems, frequently leading to violence, with no regular police-force to exercise control. Except for the sheer fact of freedom, their lives compared unfavourably with some slaves engaged in domestic duties, who were often treated almost as part of the family. Emperors and politicans did not generally think of creating job opportunities for these. The next chapter considers how they attempted to amuse those who were idle either through choice or enforced inactivity.

6

Public entertainment

Holy days and holidays

From earliest times, Roman religious tradition declared certain days of the year *dies fasti* (formal working days) and others *dies nefasti* (when business was suspended). Although the religious connexion was never forgotten, dies nefasti gradually became more like festivals or holidays as we know them. Of the 159 *dies nefasti*, fifty-nine were devoted to games (*ludi*) by the 1st century BC, rising to ninety-three under the Emperor Claudius.

THE THEATRE

The earliest form of Roman public entertainment at these festivals was the theatre. Used basically for dramatic productions, the buildings were semi-circular with a raised stage at one end. Roman playwrights admired the Greek theatre and translated Greek tragedies and comedies into Latin, adapting them for a Roman audience. There were also native Italian plays, the Atellan farces. At the festivals plays might have to compete against the performances of acrobats or jugglers. Later, dramatic productions changed in style but remained popular. Some actors, especially the 'pantomime' actors (who presented a mimed performance of dramatic scenes, accompanied by dancing and music) became the object of great public adulation, much as filmstars and pop-singers today.[1]

GLADIATORIAL SHOWS

The gladiatorial shows attracted an immense following at Rome especially after the opening of the Colosseum in AD 80, when the Emperor Titus commemorated the event with a show lasting 100 days,

---

[1]For a fuller treatment of the Roman theatre, see K. McLeish, *Roman Comedy*, in this series or *Acting and the Stage* (D. W. Taylor, Allen and Unwin).

causing a modern writer to comment:

Not until Hollywood had any single man made quite such massive and inhuman efforts to preserve his fellow man from boredom . . . Titus chose to pour a torrent of blood and treasure into the most appalling party of all time.
[J. Pearson, *Arena* p. 23]

Such horror is found in many modern writers:

It is beyond our understanding that the Roman people should have made the human sacrifice . . . a festival joyously celebrated by the whole city, or come to prefer above all other entertainment the slaughter of men armed to kill and be killed for their amusement.
[J. Carcopino, *Daily Life in Ancient Rome* p. 254]

But the games' fatal attraction is undeniable, and nowhere better illustrated than in the following passage about the Christian Alypius who attended the shows, although convinced they were disgraceful:

They arrived at the arena and sat down where they could. The place was a seething mass of frenzied and savage enthusiasm, but Alypius shut his eyes tight and told his spirit not to go near such an evil scene. If only he had been able to shut his ears as well! For when a man fell during a fight, the spectators' great roar entered his ears, and, overcome by curiosity, he opened his eyes, thinking he would be able to treat the sight with contempt. But his soul received a wound far worse than the gladiator's body . . . He saw the blood and drank in the savagery. So far from turning away, he fixed his eyes on the sight. Without understanding what was happening to him, he became frenzied; he loved the shameful struggles, drunk with blood-lust. He was no longer the man who had come to the arena, but one of the crowd.
[St. Augustine, *Confessions* VI 8]

Perhaps this mixture of hatred and excitement is possible to understand.

TYPES OF GLADIATORS

Generally, except for such types as chariot-fighters, two different kinds of gladiator were matched against each other. The main types were as follows:
Samnites. Probably the earliest gladiators, they were called after an Italian tribe defeated by the Romans. They wore heavy, splendid armour, with a large, oblong shield, leather greave (shin-guard) on the left leg, and vizored helmet with crest and plumes; their right arm had

a sleeve, and they were armed with sword or lance. Similarly equipped were the *hoplomachi.*

Thracians. These bore a curved dagger and small square or round shield; they had leather tapes round their legs and wore two greaves.

Murmillones. These replaced the *Gauls,* and were recognisable by a helmet depicting a fish. Similar to them were the *secutores.* Both had a large rectangular or oval shield and dagger or short sword. The upper part of the body was usually bare, and the legs had leather bands, with a left greave only. Round their waist was a wide metal or leather belt.

Retiarii. They had a trident or fish-harpoon, a dagger and a net (attached to a cord, to enable more than one throw to be made). The head was bare, as was the body except for a belt, loincloth, leg-bands and a shoulder-piece on the left shoulder. With this equipment resembling fishermen, they fought (appropriately) the fish-helmeted *murmillones.*

Andabatae. Dressed in chain-mail with helmets vizored but with no eye-hole, they charged blindly at each other on horse-back.

Essedarii. They were chariot-fighters, competing in horse-drawn vehicles with a driver.

ROMAN ATTITUDES

We might expect disapproval of the shows from Roman writers, but this is rare. Juvenal does object to upper-class men competing voluntarily:

Look, there's a member of the famous Gracchus family fighting . . . Just watch him hurl his net, miss the target and then run for dear life.

[Juvenal, *Satires* II 143–4]

He also attacks women who choose to take part in such games:

However can a woman keep her self-respect when her face is buried in a helmet, denying her very femininity? . . . Just watch her as she grunts and groans, bending beneath the helmet's weight, thrust and parry, her thighs enormous, swathed in bandages and tapes.   [Juvenal, *Satires* VI 418–423]

Most gladiators had no choice about fighting. Slaves, prisoners of war or condemned criminals, they lived in barracks under a trainer whose title *lanista* meant 'butcher'. Discipline was tough and punishments vicious. But gladiators were a prized possession; they had expert medical attention to keep them fit and strong. Also, as slight compen-

A retiarius

sation for a brutal life and premature death, they acquired great glamour. Juvenal is contemptuous about another phenomenon, the women who idolised gladiators:

Just *what* fired the heart of our noble Eppia? . . . His face was a frightful mess – scars from his helmet, a wart on his nose and runny eyes. *But* he was a gladiator, and that made him better than any Mr Universe. That's what she put before her husband, sister, children and country. The cold steel sends them wild.   [Juvenal, *Satires* VI 103–13]

Emperors and the shows

The spread of the shows was largely due to the emperors' sponsorship, starting with Augustus:

Augustus gave gladiatorial shows in the forum and amphitheatre . . . Sometimes the shows consisted of animal-hunts . . . there was even a sea-battle in the region of the Tiber.   [Suetonius, *Life of Augustus* 43]

Realizing that shows brightened the dreary lives of the poor and fascinated the rich, many emperors attended them regularly, and some were keen supporters. The people thus had an opportunity to see and cheer their emperor, who could show that he shared their interests.

THE COLOSSEUM

The Colosseum, most famous of Rome's monuments, was constructed largely as a piece of imperial propaganda. After the Great Fire of Rome (AD 64) had destroyed a large part of the city, Nero built himself an enormous palace, the 'Golden House'. A few years later, the emperor Vespasian took advantage of its unpopularity, had it pulled down, and began work on an enormous amphitheatre – completed the year after his death by his son Titus. The dimensions were 188 by 156 metres, and the oval arena measured eighty-six by fifty-four metres, roughly the area of four football pitches. The wooden floor was covered with sand (*arena* means 'sand') and rested on walls six metres high. Now that the floor has rotted, the whole underground network where fighters and beasts were kept before fighting has been exposed. The Colosseum seated some 45,000 to 50,000, with the *cavea* (seating-area) divided vertically into wedges (*cunei*) and horizontally into tiers. Numbers were further swollen by allowing the poor to stand in passage-ways or on the roof. The lowest tier contained reserved seats for senators and *equites*, and the Emperor's special box, the *pulvinar*. Titus was succeeded by his less popular brother Domitian. Anxious to outdo Titus' lavish shows, he staged a sea-battle (*naumachia*) on the flooded arena of the Colosseum, and provided spectacular aquatic entertainments in a special lake near the Tiber. Martial wrote poems (*The Book of Shows*), designed to flatter Domitian's arrangements. These proved popular, making Martial's name as a poet: his sentiments found an echo in many hearts:

Augustus first put on a sea-battle,
The waters stirring to the trumpet's sound.
But our emperor has wrought yet greater marvels.
Nymphs see monsters roaring in the sea . . .
Never has there been such a spectacle, sire,
In Amphitheatre or in Circus.

[Martial, *The Book of Shows*, XXVIII 1–4 9–10]

Martial fails to mention that almost all fighters and many spectators lost their lives in this fine spectacle:

Despite heavy rain and a violent storm, the emperor allowed no-one to leave or change into more suitable clothing – though he himself put on thick woollen cloaks; consequently a number fell sick and died.

[Dio Cassius, LXVII 8 2–3]

Amphitheatres were built all over the Roman world, not all as strong as they should have been, as this account shows:

A sudden disaster struck, devastating as a serious war. It was over in a moment. A freedman, Atilius, started building an amphitheatre at Fidenae for a gladiatorial show. But he had not made sure that the foundations were solid, and the wooden structure was not securely fastened . . . The fans swarmed in – men and women of all ages. The numbers were increased by the town's proximity to Rome, which made the destruction worse. The packed building collapsed, crumpling both inwards and outwards, and a huge crowd of spectators and bystanders were crushed or hurtled to their death . . .

Fifty thousand people were mutilated or crushed to death in the catastrophe. The Senate decreed that in future only those qualifying as *equites* could put on gladiatorial shows; no amphitheatres should be built unless the ground was known to provide a solid foundation. [Tacitus, *Annals* IV 62–63]

POMPEII'S AMPHITHEATRE

Something of the mania for the shows can be glimpsed from Pompeii. The town's stone amphitheatre, the first of its kind, was so solid that it

The Roman theatre at Pompeii

is still largely intact, despite time and Vesuvius. This building and the surrounding area provide much information. In the nearby gladiators' barracks were found the skeletons of six gladiators, chained together for punishment. There are also many items of graffiti, some confirming gladiators' great popularity:

The *retiarius* Crescens looks after the girls; he's their lord and master.

The shows – in one year there were forty-three days of them – were mounted by wealthy politicians seeking electoral success or showing gratitude on election, or simply for prestige. Their advertisements sometimes survive:

The troop of gladiators owned by Aulus Suettius Certus will perform at Pompeii on May 31. There will be an animal hunt; awnings will be provided.

[Awnings were canvas covers pulled over the seating-area to protect spectators from fierce weather.]

Graffiti also record the details of programmes, with results:

Thracian v. Murmillo		
Pugnax, a Neronian	(3 fights)	*Won*
Murranus, a Neronian		*Killed*
Hoplomachus v. Thracian		
Cycnus, a Julian	(8 fights)	*Won*
Atticus, a Julian	(14 fights)	*Discharged*
Chariot-fighters		
Publius Ostorius	(51 fights)	*Discharged*
Scylax, a Julian	(26 fights)	*Won*
Thracian v. Murmillo		
Lucius Fabius	(9 fights)	*Killed*
Astus, a Julian	(14 fights)	*Won*

[The number of fights shows previous victories; 'Neronian' and 'Julian' were two gladiatorial troops.]

THE START OF THE CONTESTS

Advance advertisement consisted of published lists of fighters, and heralds in the Forum. The day before the fights, contestants were given a magnificent feast by the sponsor; with macabre interest, spectators watched how they ate what was often a final meal.

The shows began with a large parade and display of fighters. When the emperor was present, they stopped before his box and cried: '*Ave, imperator, morituri te salutant*' ('Hail, Emperor, those about to die greet you').

Spectators' appetites were whetted by mock contests with dummy weapons. There might be *venationes* – wild-beast hunts in which beast-fighters (*bestiarii*) armed with hunting-spears took on such animals as elephants, panthers and lions. Then a war-trumpet announced the serious business, where men killed men. Usually, pairs of gladiators fought, sometimes teams were larger. If contestants were reluctant, trainers 'encouraged' them, assisted by slaves with whips and red-hot irons. Cowardly fighters were despised:

There were some tin-pot gladiators, so shattered before fighting that you could have knocked them down with a feather . . . Only one, a *Thracian*, had a bit of guts, but even he wasn't up to much. They were all flogged after the show because the crowds kept shouting: 'Come on, give it to them!' They were chicken! [Petronius, *Satyricon* 45]

The courage of others pleased the crowds. Cicero regarded it as an object-lesson for society:

Did you ever see even a mediocre gladiator utter a groan or register pain on his face? Which of them ever disgraced himself in his manner of falling (I won't say in fighting)? And after falling, do they flinch when the order is given for the fatal blow to be struck at their neck? That's strong discipline and training for you. And if a *Samnite*, a degraded person who deserves this kind of life, can achieve this, surely any decent man could strengthen a weakness in his character by force of training? [Cicero, *Tusculan Disputations* II 41]

THE END OF THE FIGHTS

The victorious gladiator returned to the barracks, to fight again another day. Occasionally popular fighters were granted the wooden sword, which freed them from fighting again. Many fights ended in death for one of the contestants. A loser who was not killed outright could appeal to the spectators to spare his life. Sometimes they did; otherwise they gave the sign for death – the thumb turned *up*, scholars now think; 'thumbs down' indicated mercy, the throwing away of the weapon. After fights, Negro slaves raked over the bloodstained sand. Other slaves, dressed as the god Mercury (who escorted souls to the underworld) carried bodies from the arena; those who killed seriously injured gladiators appeared as Charon, who ferried the dead into Hades.

Admiration mixed with contempt, loathing mingled with fascination – these are some Roman attitudes towards the shows. But criticism not of the gladiators but of the people who permitted, enjoyed and even worshipped them is unusual indeed. One critic was Seneca, who wrote:

Although man is sacred to man, today he is killed in sport, for sheer fun.

Another passage shows his disapproval still more clearly:

I happened to attend a lunch-time exhibition, expecting a witty, light-hearted diversion, something to take spectators' minds off the prospect of killing fellow-men. But nothing of the kind. The earlier contests had been compassionate affairs in comparison. There's no nonsense now. It's murder pure and simple. The men have no armour to protect themselves; their whole bodies are open to blows – every strike is a hit . . . When a man has killed his opponent, the spectators insist on his facing the man who will kill *him*; they think up some new kind of slaughter for the one left at the end. The only escape is death . . .

You may say: 'He was a highway robber; he killed a man.' What of it? Even if, as a criminal, *he* deserved his punishment, what crime have *you* committed to have to sit and watch it? They cry: 'Kill, flog, burn.' . . . And when there's an interval in the show, they announce: 'Let's have a few throats cut now – we must have something going on.'   [Seneca, *Letters to Lucilius* VII]

The Circuses

We turn perhaps with some relief to the Circuses and chariot-racing. We can sympathise with these more readily because of our own sporting events. If the occasional charioteer fell to a grim death beneath the wheels of the chariot or the horses' hooves, we are used to such deaths in motor-racing or hang-gliding – and they do not diminish the sport's popularity. But not all Romans loved the Circus:

Do you want to know how I've managed to enjoy blissful peace in the City during the past few days, writing and reading? The Circuses were on, a kind of show which has no appeal for me. There's no variety or novelty: see one race and you've seen them all. I can't understand why thousands of fully-grown men have such a childish passion for watching horses charging along, and men standing in chariots, over and over again. I could begin to appreciate it if they were there for the speed of the horses or the drivers' skill, but all they're really interested in is the colour of the driver's tunic – they're mad about these colours.   [Pliny the Younger, *Letters* IX 6]

The colours were popular partly because betting took place on the four teams – the major teams were Green and Blue, the minor Red and White – and partly because the teams' supporters were united by their colours, something football supporters will easily understand. Fanatical support for the teams even led to fights and rioting among the crowds – again, modern parallels readily suggest themselves. Pliny was right in stressing the colours' importance, but he exaggerated in saying that spectators were not interested in riders' skill or horses' speed. As today, people followed the races partly because of gambling, but many also had an interest in jockeys' technique and horses' racing qualities.

CIRCUS MAXIMUS

The sheer size of the Circuses made it difficult for spectators to recognise teams except by colour. The most important course in Rome was the *Circus Maximus* ('Greatest Circus'). It occupied a valley running north-west to south-east between the Aventine and Palatine Hills, an area approximately 600 metres long and 150 metres wide. First, spectators sat on the hillside or on temporary wooden seating. Gradually, more impressive, permanent buildings were erected, especially by emperors. At its largest, more than 200,000 could sit – which compares with the largest modern stadium. As in the Colosseum, the lowest (marble) tier had reserved seats; the second tier was wooden, and the highest possibly had only standing-room.

THE RACES

The chariot-races began at one end of the long course, where the huge wooden starting-gates (*carceres*) were swung open by slaves at a given signal. The horses made for the left-hand side of the central wall (*spina*). When they reached the first turning-post (*meta*) at the far end, they turned and raced back along the far side, wheeling right again to pass the near-end *meta* and complete one lap. The standard race was seven laps; lap-markers (seven bronze dolphins, and seven large stone eggs placed along the *spina*) were prominently displayed.

Some modern writers understand the allure of the races:

The Roman crowd revelled in these spectacles where everything combined to quicken their curiosity and arouse their excitement: the swarming crowd in which each was carried off his feet by all, the almost incredible grandeur of the setting . . . the powerful beauty of the stallions, . . . the perfection of their training, and above all the agility and gallantry of drivers and riders.

[J. Carcopino, *Daily Life in Ancient Rome* p. 237]

Although there were variations, the usual team was a four-horse chariot, with two central horses attached to the shaft, and two trace-horses loosely connected by the trace-rope, on the outside. On a turn, the left trace-horse was the pivot, drawn in tightly to enable the right-hand horse to swing; the outside horse was loosened on the rope sufficiently to bring the chariot round, but without swinging too wide. Failure to judge the turn correctly meant a crash against the *meta* or with the following chariot. Like the theatre and gladiatorial shows, the Circus produced wealthy and glamorous heroes. Most drivers were slaves or freedmen, but if successful they had gifts showered on them by emperors and officials, and high salaries from team-managers. One rider, Diocles, retired (after 4,257 races and 1,462 victories) with a fortune of thirty-five million sesterces. Scorpus, whose 'golden nose twinkled everywhere', according to Martial, won over 2,000 races; on his early death, Martial penned this lament:

Scorpus, robbed of your youth you are fallen.
So early, alas, you harness the black horses of Death,

Scene from a Roman chariot race. The team in the foreground is approaching the turning post

Your chariot sped its swift course to the goal.
Must your life do so too?   [Martial, X 50 5–8]

OTHER ATTRACTIONS

Other writers, like Ovid, treated the Circus more lightly. It was the
ideal opportunity to ensnare a girl:

I'm not here as a fan of these fine horses –
Though of course I hope your favourite wins.
I've come to talk to you and sit with you.
You've got to know that I'm in love with you.
You watch the races – I'm watching you.   [Ovid, *Love Poems* III 2 1 1–5]

Apart from the races and such informal entertainments, the Circus
offered *venationes*, as in the amphitheatre. There was also the public
execution of criminals, including the martyrdom of Christians – here
rather than (as is often thought) in the Colosseum. Many deaths were
theatrically staged, culminating in the mutilation and killing of the
central 'actor', a condemned criminal. Mythological scenes could thus
be portrayed with extreme realism, such as the flight of Daedalus and
Icarus which ended in tragedy when Icarus flew too near the sun and
fell into the sea:

Icarus with his dishevelled wings was hurled from the sky to break his bones in
the middle of the circus – a flight, a fall and then a mass of shapeless palpitating
flesh in a pool of blood. If Icarus finished in this way, Daedalus did not profit
from his foresight, because a ferocious beast sprang out and tore him to pieces.
The effect was magnificent, and the people abandoned themselves to trans-
ports of delight.   [U. E. Paoli, *Rome, Its People, Life and Customs* p. 252]

Martial described such a death as follows:

The quivering limbs, though lacerated, still lived,
But the body was a body no longer.
                              [Martial, *Book of the Shows* VII 5–6]

7

Private recreations

Public and private baths

For us, a bath tends to be private: not for the Romans. Wealthy men such as senators might have bathing establishments attached to their great houses, but most citizens and their wives visited public baths regularly. The emperors built luxurious bathing-establishments (*thermae*) including not only baths but an open-air exercise-area surrounded by colonnades (*palaestra*), fountains, gardens, shops, restrooms, massage-parlours, museums and libraries. Bathing establishments have been found all over the Empire. In England, Bath takes its name from them, and Pompeii had three *thermae*. Hot, dusty Italian summers made daily bathing almost a necessity, but baths were popular also for their other facilities: they provided a community sports and recreation centre. A Pompeian poet scribbled on a wall:

Wine, sex and the baths destroy our bodies.
But what makes life worth living is –
Wine, sex and the baths. [*CIL* vi 15 258]

Since brothels and bars often adjoined the baths, Pompeians could combine their pleasures easily.

VISITING THE BATHS

The baths opened about noon. Romans started work early in the morning, and continued until the heat of the day. The visit to the baths was partly a preparation for dinner (*cena*) which started in late afternoon. After a light lunch, a citizen set out, usually with a slave accompanying him. The slave carried oil-flasks to oil his master and *strigils* (blunt metal scrapers to remove dirt from the body). The Emperor Hadrian believed in bathing publicly. He had his own suites of baths, but wished to meet the people. One day he saw a veteran soldier rubbing his body against the marble wall of a bathroom. He explained to Hadrian that this was because one needed money to keep slaves – whereupon Hadrian gave him money and slaves. Next day, Hadrian saw a number of old men vigorously rubbing their backs against the wall. He told them to look after each other! Presumably this was the normal practice for the very poor, since scraping one's own back with a strigil was not exactly convenient.

On arrival, Romans paid the door-keeper a small entrance-fee (though some baths in Rome were free), and normally made for the *palaestra*, where they exercised in various ways, to keep fit and work up a sweat for the baths. (Today, on much the same principle, middle-aged businessmen dash out for a quick game of squash and a shower at lunchtime.) They ran, threw the discus, wrestled or boxed, bowled hoops (a gentle exercise favoured by women), trained with weights and played ball-games. A favourite was *trigon*. Three people formed a triangle and threw small hard balls at each other while also trying to catch those thrown at them. In Petronius' *Satyricon*, Trimalchio plays *trigon*, but as he is old and spoiled the rules are twisted:

Suddenly we saw a bald old man in a red tunic, playing *trigon* with some long-haired boys . . . The old man, exercising in his slippers, was throwing green balls around. If they touched the ground he didn't bother to pick them up; a slave stood beside him with a bagful, supplying them to the players . . . a eunuch kept score, by counting the balls dropped, not those caught.

[Petronius, *Satyricon* 27]

There was also *harpastum*, using a large ball stuffed with sand, which players had to catch while surrounded by opponents who tried to stop them; other games involved heavy medicine-balls, and inflated balls from animals' bladders.

THE BATHS THEMSELVES

Exercise finished, Romans entered the *apodyterium* (changing-room) where they deposited their clothes in niches along the wall; an attendant guarded them. The sequence of bathing varied with the facilities offered. The most splendid baths offered dry and wet heat. Bathers started in the *sudatorium*, a dry sweat-room (anticipating modern saunas) and moved to the *caldarium* where there was a large heated bath. After this came the *strigil*, applied to the opened pores; some also had a massage. Bathers then returned to the *tepidarium* (warm room) to cool off gradually, and frigidarium, a cold bath. At the Forum Baths, men proceeded from *apodyterium* to *tepidarium*,

The apodyterium *(changing-room) at the women's baths in Herculaneum. Around the walls can be seen the niches where the clothes were deposited*

gradually acclimatising themselves for the *caldarium* where, after the hot bath, they rinsed with cold water from a basin. From here they went to the *frigidarium* or, if the idea was too much for them, back to the *apodyterium*. Women did not have the option of a cold plunge.

MIXED BATHING

Not all baths had separate suites for men and women. The emperor Hadrian passed a law prohibiting mixed bathing, which shows that until then the practice had existed. Where there was only one suite, there must have been separate hours: probably women had first use.

Then men could spend most of the afternoon at the baths and adjoining facilities. Except for men like Pliny the Elder, they did not return to work; the next item on the agenda was dinner.

CENA

By this time, many were probably feeling pangs of hunger. Breakfast (*ientaculum*) and lunch (*prandium*) were light, snatched meals – some Romans skipped one or both altogether. Martial ate a little bread and cheese for breakfast; lunch might also be just bread, or cold meat, fruit or vegetables from the previous night. The day's eating and drinking centred on the *cena*.

Some people imagine the Romans indulging in enormous, interminable banquets with bizarre concoctions and exotic meats. That was true only of some of the upper classes at some periods of Rome's history. But most people ate much more simply.

DINING ARRANGEMENTS

Whether the *cena* was simple or elaborate, some features were standard for owners of a *domus* (those in *insulae* had no such formal arrangements). Meals took place in the *triclinium* (dining-room) – literally, the 'three-couch room'. The plan shows the lay-out of the three couches, and Pompeii has yielded many examples. Larger houses had a *triclinium* indoors for winter and another, open-air *triclinium* for summer, adjoining the *peristylium*. Usually, hosts sat at the position X, and the most important guests at Y. The couches, covered with mattresses for greater comfort, sloped slightly down to the front, and the three places on each couch were divided by cushions. Instead of this arrangement, a single couch for seven people, curved like a C, was sometimes used. 'Evening dress' was the *synthesis*, a long, loose-fitting gown, with embroidered decoration for the wealthy.

Diners adopted the 'reclining' position, lying forward on the couch, their left arm supported by a cushion. Holding plates in their left hand, they ate using the fingers of their right hand, or knives and spoons where necessary. They took food from a central table, round or square – often richly decorated. Other tables held later courses, displayed the family silver or accommodated extra guests such as less privileged clients.

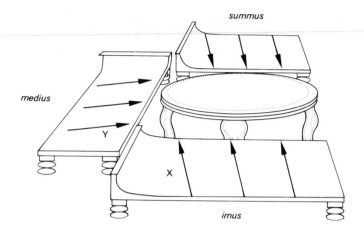

A triclinium *with places for nine guests, three to each couch. Guests reclined lying forwards, their left arm supporting their weight*

THE PLAN OF THE CENA

A standard *cena* had three courses:

1   *Gustatio* (hors d'oeuvre). Light 'appetisers', such as eggs, olives or salad-vegetables, or more elaborate items in grander banquets. This was followed by *mulsum*, wine sweetened with honey.

2   The *cena* proper. In simple meals a single meat or fish dish (or vegetables); in more luxurious dinners, successive dishes with different meats.

3   *Secundae mensae* (dessert). Fruit, nuts or simple sweet cakes. This could lead into the *comissatio*, a drinking-party with entertainment.

A master of ceremonies (*rex convivii*) decided when guests should drink, and what proportions of wine and water should be used in the mixing-bowl (*cratera*). Romans did not normally drink wine neat: proportions could be as high as four-fifths water to one-fifth wine. This explains how they survived long drinking-sessions, where the *rex convivii* fixed the number of cups each guest had to drink – normally by draining the cup in one go.

MENUS

Horace describes a simple *cena*:

Off home I go to prepare my meal: fritters, leeks and peas. Three boys serve the food; two cups and a ladle stand on a white stone slab. There is a cheap salt-cellar and an earthenware jug and saucer.   [Horace, *Satires* I 6 114–8]

Martial's dinner for seven guests is a little larger:

Lettuce, leeks and mint.
Lizard-fish garnished with sliced eggs, served with fresh herbs.
A paunch soaked in tunny-fish brine.
One young kid.
Meat-balls, beans and young sprouts.
A chicken, a ham now seeing its fourth dinner.
Ripe apples.
Wine.   [Martial, X 48 *passim*]

Juvenal compares his dinner-menu with the luxury he sees about him:

Here's what we're having – all home-grown; nothing from the market. First, a tender plump kid from my little country farm at Tivoli – the pick of the flock . . . Then wild asparagus (my bailiff's wife cut it from the hillside) . . . Good large eggs, still warm, carefully wrapped in straw; and the hen that laid them. Grapes which after six months are as fresh as when they were picked. Baskets of pears (two varieties) and apples ranking with the best orchards.
                                              [Juvenal, *Satires* XI 64–74]

But the most famous Roman dinner was Trimalchio's. Although fictitious and in some ways exaggerated, it reflects the extreme of Roman luxury in dining:

At last we reclined at table. Egyptian slave-boys poured iced water over our hands. Others followed, acting as chiropodists; they skilfully removed any loose toenails, singing all the time . . .
    Some extremely elegant hors d'oeuvres were served . . . There was a donkey of finest bronze with two panniers on his back, one with green olives, one with black . . . Small iron frames, shaped like bridges, held dormice sprinkled with honey and poppy-seeds, and there were piping hot sausages on a silver grid, with damsons and pomegranate seeds underneath.
    While we were still busy with these, a tray with a basket was brought in. On it sat a wooden hen, her wings spread wide as though broody. Two slaves ran up and (to a tune from the band) started searching through the straw. Eventually they dug out peahens' eggs and gave them to the guests. Trimalchio watched and said: 'Friends, I told that bird to sit on the eggs. I hope they're not starting to hatch – let's crack them to make sure they're still soft.' We picked up our spoons (weighing half a pound each) and cracked the eggs, which were made of rich pastry. (I'll admit I nearly threw mine away, it was so hard – thinking the baby bird was already formed.) But a guest who'd seen this

sort of thing before said: 'There'll be something good in here.' So I
investigated the shell and found a really plump little grouse, covered with
egg-yolk and seasoned with pepper . . .

Then the wine-jars, carefully sealed, were brought in, with a label reading:
OPIMIAN FALERNIAN – A HUNDRED YEARS OLD
As we examined the labels Trimalchio clapped and said, sighing: 'Wine lives
longer than we poor mortals. So let's drink. Drinking is living – and this is real
Opimian. Yesterday's guests were far classier, but they didn't get such good
wine.'   [Petronius, *Satyricon* 31–34 *passim*]

The meal continued in this extravagant vein. A late arrival, Habinnas,
had already been to one dinner-party, and Trimalchio asked him about
the food:

To start with we had a pig crowned with sausages, served with blood-puddings
and giblets (very nicely done), and beetroot and wholemeal bread, which I
prefer to white. The next course was cold tart and first-class Spanish wine
poured over hot honey. I ignored the tart and dug straight into the honey . . .

Oh yes, a piece of bear's meat was put before us. Scintilla tried it, silly girl;
she almost coughed up. But I ate more than a pound: tasted like genuine wild
boar. Well, I say that if a bear can eat a man, all the more reason for a man to
eat a bear. Finally we had cream cheese flavoured with wine, a snail each, tripe,
eggs with pastry-caps, liver, turnips, mustard. Pickled olives were passed
round in a bowl. Some greedy people took three fistfuls. We didn't bother
with the ham.   [Petronius, *Satyricon* 66]

In the circle of Pliny the Younger some doubtless enjoyed such
culinary extravaganzas. But he did not. The menu which he describes
suggests that such indulgence was exceptional:

Fancy accepting my invitation and then not coming! . . . I had the whole meal
laid out. There was one lettuce each, three snails, two eggs, barley-cake and
mulsum, chilled with snow . . . as well as olives, beetroot, gherkins, onions
and many other delicacies. You could have heard a comic actor, reader or
singer – all three if I'd been feeling generous. But you'd rather have oysters,
sea-urchins, sow's innards and Spanish dancing-girls.

[Pliny the Younger, *Letters* I 15]

One feature of many dinners aroused fierce indignation. Pliny describes it:

I happened to dine with a man (*not* a close friend) who said that he had devised
a system of 'elegant economy'; I'd call it stinginess combined with extrava-
gance. He and a chosen few received the best food; the rest got cheap bits and
pieces. He'd even put the wine into tiny flasks, so that guests could not refuse

what they were offered. The first category was for himself and us, the second for 'less important friends' (he grades his friends), the third for freedmen. The man reclining beside me asked if I approved, and I said I did not. 'What do you do, then?', he asked. 'I serve the same to everyone. I invite guests to dinner, not to divide them into classes.'   [Pliny the Younger, *Letters* II 6]

The idea was to economise when obliged to invite large numbers of clients to dinner. This could be wildly expensive if all ate extravagant food. But Pliny says: 'My freedmen do not drink my kind of wine: I drink theirs.'

Juvenal looks at the same subject from the client's viewpoint:

So after two months you are invited as the last guest – lowest position, lowest table. You're over the moon to receive the card . . . But what a dinner! The wine's worse than dishwater – just enough to get you blind drunk and immersed in brawls . . . while your host Virro drinks wine that's been lying in its jar since the consuls wore long beards . . .

And look at that enormous lobster, spreading all over the platter, piled high with a garnish of asparagus. Reserved for his lordship, that is: it looks down on the other guests. But *you* receive half an egg with a bit of crabmeat squashed up in it, on a tiny saucer – food for a ghost. *He* dresses his fish in finest oil; *you* get oil reeking of the lamp, to disguise your anaemic boiled cabbage.

[Juvenal, *Satires* V *passim*]

At the end of the meal, the clients sit silently waiting for Virro to offer them the remains of a hare, or scraps from the wild boar. But there is no joy; the evening trails to a pathetic conclusion.

COMISSATIO

It was possibly a late conclusion, too – a *comissatio* could go on past midnight. While the guests drank, slaves provided cabaret. Dancing-girls were popular, although traditionally-minded Romans despised dancing. A Roman senator was horrified to see children learning to dance:

I swear I saw over fifty boys and girls, including a boy no more than twelve, and the son of a candidate for the consulship, dancing with castanets. The sight made me despair for Rome's future: the lowest kind of slave would shrink from performing such a dance.   [Macrobius, III 14–7]

But if it was improper for guests to dance themselves, it was another matter to watch slaves dancing. Not all slaves shrank from such dances: one mosaic shows a female dancer in a decidedly see-through dress. Juvenal, like Pliny, regarded this as inferior entertainment:

If you're expecting Spanish dancing-girls with castanets, you've got the wrong address . . . Such debauchery is for the rich. Gambling and adultery are quite the done thing for them, but not for us. Our dinner will have a nobler entertainment. We'll hear Homer's tale of Troy, and Virgil's fine poem, a rival even for Homer. [Juvenal, *Satires* XI 171–181 (with omissions)]

Intellectuals' dinner-parties contained poetry-recitations, comic actors – and conversation: good conversation was the essence of civilized eating and drinking. For those with less elevated tastes, dancers were joined by acrobats, clowns or dwarfs – whose very appearance was an entertainment for many Romans, though the act was enhanced by juggling or tumbling.

Various entertainments

Or the evening might produce dice or knucklebones. Interest was enlivened by betting; even emperors participated. Suetonius records a letter written by Augustus:

Yesterday and today we gambled like old men, at dinner. We played knucklebones; anyone who threw ones or sixes put a coin in the pool. A 'full house' scooped the pool. [Suetonius, *Life of Augustus* 71]

Two Roman women playing a game with knucklebones

For knucklebones the Romans used the *talus*, a small bone from animals, between the shin and ankle-bone. There were four marked surfaces, numbered 1, 3, 4 and 6. These gave thirty-five possible combinations; the best throw, the 'full house', was the *Venus*, where each piece showed a different number. Dice were precisely like ours, with six numbered faces.

Such games were played by children and adults, as were games with boards and pieces or counters. One popular game, like backgammon, was *ludus duodecim scriptorum* (the twelve-piece game); many boards with various patterns survive. Moves were determined by throwing dice. Children's games included 'odds and evens', where one player had to guess whether the other held an odd or even number of objects in his hand, spinning tops, Blind Man's Buff and skipping.

AFTER THE CENA

When guests finally emerged, the fortunate had slaves to light their way home, in the absence of street-lighting. Journeys could be hazardous:

The drunken young bully keeps well away from the rich man in his scarlet cloak, surrounded by torches, big brass lamps and a large bodyguard. It's the man like me he's waiting for, walking back alone by moonlight or with hand cupped round the wick of a sputtering candle . . . If you're lucky, when he's finished battering you he'll leave you a few teeth . . . Or you might meet a robber. Houses locked up, shops with shutters down – it's the ideal time. Perhaps a mugger will spring out with a knife and have a go at you – the City's full of cut-throats.   [Juvenal, *Satires* III 288–308 (with omissions)]

Inns and bars

Most guests presumably survived to eat another day. Not every day carried shows or dinner-invitations, and informal entertainment often centred on *popinae* or *tabernae* – snack-bars and inns. These sold hot and cold snacks and drinks, and some offered a sit-down dinner or overnight stay to travellers. An inscription records a conversation between an innkeeper and her guest:

'Innkeeper, let's work out the bill.'
'One pint of wine and bread, one *as*. Food, two *asses*.'
'Agreed.'

'Girl's services, eight *asses*.'
'Agreed, again.'
'Hay for the mule, two *asses*.'
'That mule will ruin me!'   [*ILS* 7478]
[The *as* was a small copper coin: sixteen *asses*=four sesterces=one *denarius*]

The room, it appears, came with the girl – or the girl with the room.

Often inns were gambling-dens, as illustrations from one in Pompeii show, with the characters speaking in the world's first 'cartoon balloons':

Scene one: Two men greet each other on meeting.
Scene two: A barmaid, with jug and beaker, serves the men:
    Barmaid: Whose drink is this? Come on, Oceanus, drink up!
    First man: Here.
    Second man: No, it's mine.
Scene three: The men sit gambling at a table, with *ludus duodecim scriptorum*:
    First man: I'm out.
    Second man: That's a two, not a three.
Scene Four: The landlord intervenes as they are about to come to blows:
    First man: You low-down son of a bitch!
    Landlord: Outside, if you're going to quarrel.

Travellers sometimes recorded their appreciation of a visit, on the walls:

Good work, innkeeper, you found me a seat.

If they were having trouble getting service, they wrote up their request:

Another cup of Setian wine.   [*CIL* iv 1292]

And some were far from satisfied:

Damn you, innkeeper, selling water and drinking neat wine yourself!
                                                         [*CIL* iv 3948]
Which reminds us that not all Romans were as dignified as Pliny the Younger, or spent their days and nights like Pliny the Elder!

8

Religion

At midnight the worshipper arises. His feet are bare; he makes a sign, his thumb between closed fingers, in case some bodiless spirit should meet him through the silence. He washes his hands in spring water; he turns, takes up black beans and throws them away, his face averted. As he throws, he says: 'These I cast. With these I purify myself and my own.' He repeats this nine times, without looking back; the spirit is thought to gather the beans, following behind, unseen. Once again he touches water, clashes bronze and asks the spirit to leave his house. Nine times he repeats: 'Ghosts of my fathers, go forth.' Then he looks back, believing he has duly carried out the rites.

[Ovid, *Fasti* V 429–444]

The procession of the saviour goddess began. Women in white robes, with wreaths of spring flowers on their heads and arrayed in jewels, scattered petals on the ground. Others held bright mirrors behind their backs, turning them reverently towards the passing goddess . . .

A crowd of men and women came with lamps, firebrands and wax torches. They worshipped Isis, daughter of the heavenly stars, with these man-made lights. Then came the sound of beautiful music on pipes and flutes, and a chosen chorus of youths, dressed for the festival in white clothes, sang a lovely hymn . . . Now the multitudes of initiates poured in, those who knew the sacred mysteries: men and women of all classes and ages, conspicuous in their pure white linen robes. The women's hair was oiled and covered in bright cloth; the men's heads were completely shaven, their bald heads shining like stars on earth, to honour this wonderful religion. They shook bronze, silver and gold rattles which made a high, tinkling sound.

[Apuleius, *The Golden Ass* XI 9–10]

These two passages depict religious ceremonies. First, Ovid, in a long poem about the origins of the Roman calendar, explores primitive religious traditions. There is an atmosphere of dark superstition. In the second, from a novel by Apuleius, the impression is one of bright, joyous worshippers: everything is light and blissful.

Religion means different things to different people, but its influence is vast. Not only Roman poets, but historians, orators and biographers contain references to religion, superstition, magic or witchcraft on almost every page. This chapter looks briefly at the various forms of religious belief and practice which influenced the Roman world. These ranged from grand public ceremonies to small, private observances.

Rome's religious origins

Stories of Rome's beginnings were full of gods and heroes, as the historian Livy found:

The presence of the gods gives the past a certain dignity, and if any nation deserves to be allowed to claim that its ancestors were gods, that people is our own. [Livy, *History*, Preface]

The founder was Romulus, son of the god Mars and a mortal Rhea Silvia, according to legend. Even before Romulus, stories told of Aeneas, who escaped from Troy after the Trojan War, and founded an Italian city, Rome's predecessor. Aeneas, too, was the son of a divine parent – the goddess Venus – and the mortal Anchises.

Rome inherited many myths and legends – even gods and goddesses – from the Greeks. By a change of name, Zeus became Jupiter and Hera, his wife, Juno. In fact, the whole Greek 'pantheon', with twelve major gods and goddesses, was taken over and worshipped by the Romans. These gods were at the heart of the official religion observed throughout the Roman Empire.

ROMAN STATE RELIGION

Such worship took place in Rome's many temples. At one end of the *Forum Romanum* was the temple of Vesta and house of the Vestal Virgins. Next door was the Chief Priest's house, and nearby the Temple of Castor and Pollux, opposite the Temple of Saturn. There were also the Temple of Julius Caesar, the Sacred Spring of Juturna, the Portico of the Twelve Gods, and several others. On the Palatine Hill over a dozen temples have been identified, including one to the strangely-named goddess 'Fever', and another to Viriplaca, a goddess who acted as marriage-guidance counsellor. Nearby, on the Capitoline Hill, the 'great gods' had their centre, the temple of *Jupiter Capitolinus*, associated in worship with Juno and Minerva.

The state gods were offered animal sacrifices at the altars, on festival days and at times of national crisis. Ordinary people thought that the gods would protect the city if the magistrates and priests kept up such sacrifices. They did not need to worry much themselves, and were content that the temples (housing the god's images) should be closed for most of the year.

VESTAL VIRGINS

At the centre were the Vestal Virgins. The writer Cicero echoed the official attitude when he said that 'if the gods did not hear the Vestal Virgins' prayers, the state would not survive'. The rules governing their selection were strict:

A girl cannot be chosen under six or more than ten years old; her father and mother must be alive; she must have no speech-impediment, hearing-defect or other physical weakness, and her father must not have surrendered his legal control over her.   [Aulus Gellius, *Attic Nights* I 12 1]

Their primary function was to keep alight the sacred flame in the Temple of Vesta (goddess of the hearth). The site of this temple was

The Roman goddess Vesta, who was served by the Vestal Virgins

held in great awe. Tacitus records an incident concerning Nero:

> Nero went to the Capitoline Hill to consult the gods about a journey. He worshipped the Capitoline gods, then entered the Temple of Vesta. Suddenly all his limbs started trembling. He was frightened by the goddess. Or perhaps he was always frightened, remembering his crimes. Anyway, he abandoned the journey.
>
> [Tacitus, *Annals* XV 36]

The Vestal Virgins took turns to guard the sacred flame. Despite the danger of the fire setting alight the whole temple (as great as the risk of its going out), they could not use canal or river water, only holy water from a special spring. One Virgin carried this on her head in a jar (specially constructed so that it would not stand upright) and placed it in a marble tank. If she put it down on the way, the water lost its holiness. There were six Virgins, who served for thirty years. Naturally, they were pledged to remain virgins. A Vestal who lost her virginity was buried alive in an underground chamber. (In early times the guilty man was flogged to death with his head between a wooden fork.) However there were compensations, the office carried great prestige. Apart from the Emperor's wife, they were the only women allowed to travel in a carriage in Rome; in court they did not swear an oath; and there were splendid banquets and vast State subsidies. Many stayed on after their thirty-year period: Junia Torquata served for 64 years, a record.

CHIEF PRIEST AND PRIESTS

The Vestal Virgins' only superior was the Chief Priest (*Pontifex Maximus*). Julius Caesar held this important office, which helped his political career greatly. He moved from a relatively poor family home to the fine mansion in the *Forum*. The emperors, following Augustus' lead, took the position themselves – fearing its power or wanting its prestige. Under the Chief Priest came not only the Vestal Virgins, but also a body of sixteen priests. These were not at all like present-day parish priests or clergymen; they simply presided over the State religious sacrifices and gave advice to magistrates on religious matters.

PROPHECY AND DIVINATION

Closely associated with the priests was another body of sixteen men, the *augures*. At sacrifices, these specially appointed men interpreted the omens – signs of divine approval or disapproval. Cicero was an *augur*, and he wrote a long work about the varieties of observation (*divinatio*). There were three basic categories:

1 Signs from animals or humans. Soothsayers studied the flight of birds or inspected the entrails (especially the liver) of sacrificial victims, such as chickens. Any abnormal size or colour was a bad omen. So were some human movements such as twitching or sneezing.

2 Inanimate objects. Divine power was thought to guide the fall of dice or knucklebones; or books were opened at random, and the words regarded as prophetic.

3 Unusual natural events. Storms, earthquakes or meteorites, and freak births (a five-legged calf, for instance) were thought to herald great political changes.

As well as the official *augures*, divination was also practised by many other soothsayers, and private individuals could seek advice on whether or not they should go ahead with an intended project. Alternatively, they could consult prophets or prophetesses. Among these were the Sibyls, women who uttered weird sounds which interpreters then wrote down. Collections of the sayings of the Sibyls were sometimes consulted officially.

EMPEROR-WORSHIP

State-religion changed under the Emperors. Once the dead Julius Caesar was deified, Augustus was a god's son (*divi filius*) by adoption. It was a short step to becoming a god himself. Apart from emperors whose memories were officially condemned (like Caligula and Nero), deification on death became the normal thing, prompting Vespasian's dying words: 'I think I'm turning into a god!' Romans took a time to get used to worshipping living emperors, but subjects in Eastern countries (accustomed to regarding kings as divine) began emperor-cults, which spread to the West. Emperors accepted 'divinity' because it could strengthen their position. But to many Romans the idea of worshipping a living man remained ludicrous.

Other forms of worship

THE HOUSEHOLD GODS

To most Romans, then, the official state-religion simply existed, and its requirements were few. Far closer to their hearts was the worship which a family carried out within its own home. Here, the gods were not the 'great gods' who protected the State, but the gods offering personal protection. Apart from Vesta, the *Lares* and *Penates* protected the household and store-cupboard; the *genius*, represented artistically as a huge serpent, guarded one family exclusively. In the *atrium* was a shrine (*lararium*), where prayers and sacrifices were offered. On some shrines found at Pompeii were trays for food and drink. It was believed that gods took what they required, and humans could then consume the food.

The new religions

CHRISTIANITY

But even the household worship often lacked real personal satisfaction for the worshippers, and many people turned instead to various new religions which spread to the city. These attracted followers partly because believers felt that they were a specially privileged group. Of these religions the one which has had by far the most permanent effect is Christianity, which reached the city by Claudius' reign. It is clear that by the time the apostle Paul arrived, there were Christians there to greet him:

The Christians at Rome had heard about us and came out to Appii Forum and Tres Tabernae to meet us. When Paul saw them he gave thanks to God and took courage. [Saint Luke, *Acts of the Apostles* 28 15]

Christians had a hard time at Rome. The first persecution followed the Great Fire of Rome:

Nothing men could do removed the suspicion that the fire had been started deliberately. To suppress these rumours, Nero produced scapegoats, and punished in every possible way the Christians (this was their nickname), well-known for their wickedness . . . First Nero had self-confessed Christians arrested. Then, on their information, many others were condemned, not so much for fire-raising as because of hatred of the human race. Their deaths became farces. They were dressed in wild animal-skins, and torn to pieces by dogs, or crucified, or made into torches to provide artificial daylight after dark. [Tacitus, *Annals* XV 43–44]

Perhaps Paul and Peter (who, according to tradition, was crucified hanging upside-down) died at this time. But persecution did not wipe out Christianity. Christians met secretly in the catacombs, tunnels beneath the City, and gained in numbers. Their strength came largely from their conviction that Jesus gave them salvation and eternal life if they stayed loyal even under torture. They attracted followers from slaves and lower classes, but also intellectuals and senators. Two centuries after Tacitus wrote, the Emperor Constantine became a Christian. Christianity became Rome's official religion and its leader (the Pope) took the title of *Pontifex Maximus*.

THE WORSHIP OF ISIS

The goddess Isis came to Rome from Egypt – in Egyptian mythology she was a daughter of the sun-god Ra and wife of Osiris. Romans were attracted to the ancient myth, with its stories of love and sacrifice, death and resurrection. Like Christianity, it produced in its followers a deep personal commitment; but unlike Christianity, the central figure was a remote, legendary character from the distant past. The descrip-

A wall-painting from Pompeii showing a ceremony in the worship of the goddess Isis. (Notice the bald-headed priests with their flowing white robes)

79

tion by Apuleius (see page 73) is of the Festival of Isis. This was held on 5 March every year to commemorate the return of spring, and was the central ceremony in the worship. The passages shows that the worship was accompanied by important cult-objects – special dress and sacred rattles. The ceremonies also included hymns, readings from sacred texts, secret societies and the interpretation of dreams.

THE WORSHIP OF MITHRAS

Mithras was a Persian god whose titles included 'Lord of Light', 'Giver of Happiness', 'Victorious' and 'Warrior'. He was especially popular with Roman soldiers. His worship (confined to men) took place all over the Empire. This was another religion offering the hope of a happy life beyond the grave, and there were secret rites. Followers progressed through seven stages of initiation: Raven, Bride, Soldier, Lion, Persian, Messenger of the Sun, and Father. They underwent ordeals and ate ceremonial meals, as did the Christians with their Love Feast or Holy Communion. Mithras' temples were designed as caves, from the cave where Mithras killed the bull, symbolising the triumph of good over evil, light over darkness.

MYSTERY-RELIGIONS

Similar 'mystery-religions' were widespread. They were all reserved for initiates, and shared a belief in the afterlife for the faithful. This was the important difference from the official state-religion – which offered no such comfort; people no longer took seriously the myths of Hades and Charon:

Today not even children, except those so small they get into the baths free, believe the nonsense about ghosts, underground kingdoms and rivers, with black frogs croaking in the Styx, and thousands of corpses rowed across in a tiny boat.   [Juvenal, *Satires* III 149–152]

SUPERSTITIONS

Just as many turned for personal satisfaction from the official religions to new cults, so others took seriously a variety of superstitious beliefs and practices. The use of superstition in the official sacrifices no doubt encouraged the spread of more unofficial forms.

ASTROLOGERS

One group to take advantage of this were the astrologers, with their belief in the effect of the stars on mankind. Remembering how seriously horoscopes in newspapers are taken today, it is not surprising that astrologers were extremely influential. Even some emperors were attracted, although others expelled them from the city as a threat to the official religion:

Tiberius asked the astrologer Thrasyllus if he had read his own horoscope for the present year and day. Thrasyllus made calculations based on the position of the stars and their relation to each other. He hesitated, then showed fear. The closer he looked, the greater his astonishment and terror. He cried that he was facing a crisis which might prove fatal. Tiberius clasped him warmly, congratulated him on anticipating his danger and assuring him that he would escape it.   [Tacitus, *Annals* VI 21]

[Tiberius secretly killed astrologers who did not convince him of their powers.]

CURSES AND SPELLS

Romans also tried to influence the future by magic and spells, especially curses (*defixiones*), written on lead tablets and hung on walls. These were often written by rejected lovers; some were extremely violent:

O gods of the underworld, break and smash her bones, choke her, *arourarely-oth*, let her body be twisted and shattered, *phrix*, *phrox*.

The curses often included such magical nonsense words, as well as magic signs and pictures of underworld demons.

SORCERESSES

Some women, rejected in love, turned instead to sorcery, using magic potions with standard ingredients of a witch's brew – frogs' intestines, owls' feathers, snakes' bones, herbs and poisons. Such spells and potions were also used for medicinal prophecy.

GHOSTS

Rome had many superstitions dealing with ghosts and 'foul fiends'.

Pliny describes a 'traditional' ghost:

> At Athens there was a large, spacious house with a reputation for being haunted, dangerous for inhabitants. At the dead of night the clank of iron and, if you listened carefully, the rattle of chains could be heard – first in the distance, then getting closer. The ghost appeared – an old man, his features drawn, filthy dirty, with long straggling beard and hair on end. He had fetters on his legs and manacles on his wrists, which he shook.
>
> [Pliny the Younger, *Letters* VII 27]

Finally, a philosopher discovered that a man's body lay in the garden, covered in chains, and not properly buried. After a public burial, the ghost was laid.

Telling ghost-stories could be an after-dinner entertainment. At Trimalchio's dinner-party one guest described a werewolf: a man passing a graveyard at night took off his clothes (which turned to stone), became a wolf and rushed howling into the woods. Trimalchio followed this with a story of a witch stealing a baby and substituting a straw-dummy, and injuring a strong slave:

> These midnight hags, who could turn night to day, exist all right. And the big chap? Well, he never recovered: went mad a few days later and died.
>
> We were astonished and convinced; we kissed the table, begging the midnight hags to stay at home till we got back from dinner.
>
> [Petronius, *Satyricon* 63–64]

Greek philosophy

But if intellectuals were satisfied neither by official or new religions, nor by superstition and magic, they could always study the ideas of Greek philosophy, and many did. As in many other areas, the Romans were strongly influenced by the achievements of the Greeks. Cicero spent much of his life trying to express ideas found in Greek philosophy in the Latin language, and two 'schools' of philosophy in particular found great favour in Rome.

STOICISM

The founder of this philosophical 'school', Zeno, taught in a 'stoa' (colonnade) in Athens in the fourth century BC. Stoics took from him the belief that all men were brothers, an idea which challenged accepted ideas on slavery, for instance. They also felt that it was important for men to live in accordance with nature; this would enable them to follow the divine will. Whatever sufferings Fate might send must be accepted without complaining. Today, this resigned endurance of pain is still called 'stoical'. The writer who did most to spread Stoic ideas at Rome was Seneca. He wrote a series of letters to a friend in which he often stressed the importance of philosophy (by which he meant Stoic philosophy particularly):

The one task of philosophy is to discover the truth about the divine and human worlds. It is always concerned with religion, piety, justice and all the other associated (and inseparable) virtues. Philosophy has taught men to worship what is divine, to love what is human. It tells us that power belongs to gods, and that men should have fellowship among themselves . . . Philosophy aims to make men reach happiness, and guides us towards that goal, showing us the difference between real and apparent evils . . . Philosophy gives men understanding of the whole of nature, and of wisdom itself.

[Seneca, *Letters to Lucilius* XC 3 28]

Certainly Seneca's Stoic beliefs appear to have helped him to endure suicide when he fell from the favour of Nero.

EPICUREANISM

The rival school was Epicureanism, called after the Greek philosopher Epicurus who also taught in Athens, a little later than Zeno. Today, the word 'epicure' suggests a person devoted to expensive tastes, particularly in eating. But this use is misleading. Epicureans believed in a simple life. The happiness of the soul was more important than bodily pleasures. In this respect their ideas were not completely different from Stoic philosophy, and Seneca often quotes from the writings of Epicurus. Epicurean philosophy also dealt with scientific questions. Epicurus himself believed in an 'atomic' theory of the creation of the universe. First, he thought, there had been shapeless atoms, but these had combined to form sky, air, sea and earth. Later came plants and animals, all by natural forces. The gods had no part in these processes. In Roman times, the poet Lucretius, in a long work called *The Nature of the Universe*, did much to make Epicurean ideas popular.

Pietas and the family

Beneath all the various forms of religious, superstitious or philosophical expressions there lay a basic Roman idea, for which the Latin word is *pietas*. This word cannot properly be translated into English by a single word. It stands for all the duties a Roman felt towards his gods, his country, his friends and – perhaps above all – to members of his family, alive or dead. For this reason, the traditions associated with life's critical stages give a clear picture of some aspects of *pietas*, one of the most basic forms of religious observance.

BIRTH

When a child was born in a rich man's family, a senior maidservant informed him, as head of the house (*paterfamilias*). He then decided whether to recognise the child as his, by picking it up from the ground where it had been placed. Otherwise, the child could not become part of the family, and the unwanted child was 'exposed' to die. Most unwanted children were girls: they could not continue the family line, and their births were greeted less enthusiastically. (Writers expressed few qualms about 'exposure'; under the later emperors, however, it was regarded legally as murder.) If the child *was* accepted, this was the signal for celebration. Wreaths hung on doorposts announced the arrival.

On the ninth day of a boy's life (eighth for a girl) came the *dies lustricus* (day of purification), when babies were named, with prayers for health and happiness. The eldest son usually took all his father's three names, *praenomen*, *nomen* and *cognomen*; later sons had a different *praenomen*. The *praenomen* was usually abbreviated to one letter (T. for Titus, M. for Marcus); the *nomen* was the tribal name and the *cognomen* the family's own name. Girls usually received only one name, a feminine form of the *nomen*. Thus the orator M. (Marcus) Tullius Cicero had a son, M. Tullius Cicero, and a daughter Tullia. The *dies lustricus* was a major family event, celebrated by friends and clients. Presents were brought and the *bulla*, a golden amulet, hung round the neck as a lucky charm.

The child was firmly under the father's authority. Fathers were originally entitled by law to kill children, but gradually this strictness relaxed; later writers even talk of fathers being too permissive. Boys of about 16 were released from the father's authority by the coming-of-age ceremony. The boy removed the *bulla* and adopted the plain white toga of adult citizens, except for senators; this replaced the *toga praetexta* with its purple fringe.

MARRIAGE

Depending on the marriage-contract, girls either passed into their husband's authority or remained permanently under their father's. The latter was more informal, and more easily ended; it became very popular. However, some upper-class families retained the traditional rituals.

The marriage was called *confarreatio*, after the sharing of a wheaten cake, a central ceremony. First, the betrothal had been arranged by the girl's father and her future husband – she did not necessarily even know the name of her betrothed. Afterwards, she received a gold ring from the man, now her fiancé. Girls commonly married at fourteen or fifteen: eligible brides were snapped up quickly. The contract involved the dowry, an often substantial gift from father to bridegroom.

The wedding-day was chosen carefully, avoiding such ill-omened times as May. The second half of June was better: Juno was the protectress of marriage. There were many preparations. The day before the wedding, the girl offered her toys to the family *Lares*, and went to bed in her wedding-dress with its flame-coloured veil. Slaves then decorated the house with wreaths of flowers, coloured ribbons and laurel-branches, and placed carpets at the entrance.

For the wedding-day, the bride had a special hair-do, with specially selected ribbons which she had never worn before; six locks of hair were parted with a special iron spear. The long, belted dress was plain white; a veil covered her face, and she wore yellow shoes. A matron of honour attended her.

The ceremony began with sacrifices and inspecting the omens. For society weddings, the Chief Priest presided. Witnesses watched the signing of the contract, and the matron of honour placed the couple's right hands in each other. They made silent vows, and offered the wheat-cake to the priest to bless.

A banquet followed, and the bride was conducted to her husband's home. He seized her and whisked her away from her protesting mother – commemorating the first Romans' seizure of their wives, the Sabine women. The procession set off, the bride carrying the spindle and distaff which symbolised her responsibilities, and accompanied by three boys. One had a hawthorn torch, and gave the charred remains of this to guests for luck. Crowds followed shouting *talasse* and rude jokes (both thought to be lucky). On arrival the bride decorated the doorway with woollen strips and anointed it with oil. The husband went into the house and asked her name, to which she replied '*Ubi tu Gaius, ego Gaia*' ('Where you are Gaius, I am Gaia'). Members of the procession carried the bride over the threshold. In another ceremony, the two shared fire and water and prepared for the 'first night' with

A Roman matron, wearing the stola *(dress) and* palla *(long cloak)*

fertility-rites, while the matron of honour made the marriage-bed ready. Guests watched the husband remove the girl's cloak and undo the special knot on her belt, then withdrew.

Next day, for the first time the girl wore a married women's clothing: simple underclothes (the plain brassière, *strophium*, and possibly a loincloth), a tunic, dress, *stola*, and *palla*, a long cloak for outdoor wear.

Many of these details come from a poem by Catullus, constructed as a hymn to the god of marriage, Hymen. He invites this god to participate in an imagined wedding-day:

O Hymen, cover your brow with sweet-smelling marjoram, take the flame-coloured veil, come joyfully, wearing yellow shoes on your snow-white feet; excited by this happy day, sing the wedding-song in a ringing voice. Stamp on the ground and shake the pinewood torch.

The poem ends with a prayer that the marriage will be blessed with children:

I pray to see a tiny Torquatus stretching his delicate hands from his mother's lap, and smiling sweetly at his father with lips half-open.

[Catullus, *Poems* 61 5–15 209–213]

Roman rituals concerned with death were equally complex. Although burials took place outside city-walls (burial inside the city was sacrilege), the dead were by no means ignored. Mourning and grief were expressed openly – the Romans even designed a flask to measure a widow's weeping.

Traditionally, a close relation tried to catch the dying man's final breath with a kiss, then close his eyes. All present shouted the dead man's name, and careful preparations for burial began. The body was washed and anointed to help prevent decay (a rich man's body might lie unburied for a week), and dressed in fine clothes, then placed on a special couch in the *atrium*, surrounded by flowers, wreaths and candles. The hearth-fire was extinguished in mourning. Women kept up a continual lament, beating breasts and tearing hair and clothes.

The poor had little ceremony at all – their bodies were quietly buried by night in public cemeteries. But a wealthy man's funeral was announced by a herald, and undertakers were hired. Torch-bearers and hired mourners headed the procession, which included clowns and dancers singing and joking – a religious tradition not thought to spoil the ceremony. Pliny the Elder records an important ingredient:

Wax portraits were made as images to accompany the family's funeral processions. So whenever someone died, every member of the family who had ever existed was present.   [Pliny the Elder, *Natural History* XXXV 2]

Tombs lining a street outside the gates of Pompeii

An array of mourners wore these portrait-heads, dressed in the ancestors' grandest clothes, to show their status. Sometimes these 'ancestors' stood in chariots, and sometimes slaves held them head-high on open coffins.

The uncovered corpse lay on a coffin behind the ancestors. Finally came the living family-mourners. The whole procession moved to the burial-site for the cremation or burial. For cremation, the corpse was placed on a funeral-pyre. His eyes were opened and closed and a final kiss was given. Afterwards, the mourners poured wine over the ashes, and placed them in the urn. This urn, or the coffin in the case of burial, was placed in a family tomb with a suitable inscription (*epitaph*).

The funeral did not end interest in the dead man's welfare. It was important to look after the ghost, partly to prevent haunting. Tombs lined the streets outside city-gates, some as large as houses, with small flower-gardens. With the dead man were buried things he might need for whatever future existence he had – food and drink, clothing and tools. The dead were thought to drink blood, and Romans substituted wine, pouring it through special holes into the tombs. Anniversary banquets were also supposed to cheer up the dead.

The epitaphs (some simple, others formal) have been of great value to scholars and archaeologists, but they are often interesting in themselves, as they record the *pietas* of the writers. The first is from a widower to his dead wife:

Friends, I have not much to say. Stop and read it.
This is the grave – not beautiful, but of a beautiful woman.
Her parents named her Claudia.
She loved her husband from her heart.
She had two sons.
One she leaves on earth,
The other she has placed beneath the earth.
Her speech was charming, her conduct was fitting.
She kept house, she spun wool.
I've finished. Go now.   [*CIL* I 2 1211]

The second shows that *pietas* could extend beyond the immediate family:

To the spirits of the departed.
Marcus Canuleius Zosimus lived twenty-eight years.
A patron erected this for his well-deserving freedman.
While he lived he spoke badly of no-one;

He did nothing without his patron's consent.
He had much gold and silver in his trust,
But he never wished to possess it.
At his craft, engraving silver plate, he had no equal.   [*CIL* VI 9 222]

9

Conclusion

'Comparisons are odious', it has been said. They certainly can be when the intention is to pour scorn, or when chalk is being compared with cheese. Many people compare the variety, amenities and economic prosperity of Roman life with our own, but this can be meaningless. There is little point in saying: 'I would not have liked to live in Roman times because they had no football, television or cars.' Neither did they have hydrogen bombs, widespread lung cancer and coronary thrombosis, severe pollution of seas and rivers or many other disagreeable aspects of our 'civilization'.

But it may be worth asking whether (given obvious technical limitations) the Romans produced a satisfying and enjoyable way of living. Only those who live in a society could really answer such questions, and only the fabled time-traveller could interrogate those who scrawled their comments on the walls of Pompeii, or erected tombstones to a beloved wife – or who left no memorial: the silent majority, whose viewpoint would be fascinating.

However, throughout this book a number of Romans *have* spoken, in what they wrote. Reading such passages, someone has suggested that one might be forgiven for thinking that the Romans were 'a band of permissive libertines with no shame or scruple, with a few sour-faced, censorious old so-and-sos making snide comments in between'. Of course, any selection of writers can only contribute a part of the whole story. Maybe poets such as Juvenal and Martial do spend a long time grumbling about their society; and perhaps Seneca and Pliny the Younger sometimes seem too good to be true. But many signs of real enjoyment of life come through. Even Juvenal enjoyed his grumbles, and Seneca his Stoic suffering.

All of them could enjoy life in peace. After Civil Wars brought the Republic to an end, Augustus introduced a period of untroubled stability for most of the Empire which lasted for centuries. Our era has been less fortunate.

The price for peace was the rule of the emperors. Traces of former

'Republican' freedom remained: people learned to argue 'Down with the Tyrant', and local elections at Pompeii were keenly fought. But there were no guarantees against cruel or mad emperors. Nero forced Seneca to commit suicide; Christians met hideous deaths in the public shows which showed a vein of cruelty running through Roman life. Emperors could kill their subjects, masters their slaves; fathers – in theory at least – their sons. Such violent attitudes, as well as many examples of 'permissive' behaviour, look very familiar.

But within the system there could be loyalty, friendship, affection. Not all emperors were greedy for power; some were hardworking and intelligent. There were plenty of kind masters who freed slaves, and many happy, united families. Writers referred constantly to *humanitas* (respect for other human beings). When Pliny the Younger refused to treat freedmen differently from wealthy guests at dinner, he was by no means exceptional.

Under the emperors, citizens from towns all over the Empire were urged to live at peace with each other, and many came to regard themselves as living in a vast common fatherland. From Scotland to Iraq, the territories of the Roman Empire have never been re-united since the Empire's fall. But the Roman Empire has passed on to future generations not only its buildings, roads and other proofs of military triumph. It also originated and handed down to posterity what many consider its greatest contribution, Roman law. In addition, it has transmitted two powerful forces, neither of which the Romans originated. One is Greek philosophy, from which much modern philosophical and even scientific thinking derives. The other, Christianity, passed from rejection and persecution to official recognition and benediction. Rome still remains the centre of the Christian church with the largest membership. The Bible was translated into Latin. Church services have used the Latin language until the twentieth century. Although Latin is often called a dead language, this is not entirely true. Since the time of the Romans there has been an unbroken tradition of speaking, reading and writing Latin.

This would not, perhaps, have surprised some Romans. They did not expect the Roman world to collapse, ever. *Aeternitas* (eternity) became a motto. Virgil, in his national epic, showed what he thought would bring the Romans immortality:

Others, I believe, will hammer out with greater delicacy
Living likenesses from bronze, or be greater orators.
Others will measure the movements of the heavens,

And tell the rising of the constellations.
But remember, o Roman, to guide nations with your imperial power
(This will be your special skill), and to bring peace and civilization,
Defeating the arrogant in battle and sparing the conquered.

[Virgil, *Aeneid* VI 847–53]

On a more down-to-earth note, the anonymous scribblers were not
concerned about the fall of Rome when they wrote such carefree lines
as these:

Want my advice? There's too much money in the Treasury. Share it out!

I've just won 855 sesterces at dice – and no cheating!

And, despite the gloomy opening, the walls of Pompeii *have* preserved
for ever the following poem from an unknown hand:

Nothing can last for ever.
The sun shines gold
But it must plunge into the sea.
The moon gleamed so brightly
But it has disappeared.
One day your beloved rages furiously
But the storm will yield to the gentle west wind.

Bibliography

First and foremost, the ancient authors – especially Juvenal, Martial and Pliny the Younger. Also, the poems of Horace, Virgil, Catullus and Ovid; the histories of Livy and Tacitus; the biographies of Suetonius and Plutarch; the letters of Cicero and Seneca; and the novels of Petronius and Apuleius. See also the collections of source-materials in *Roman Civilisation* (Lewis and Reinhold, 2 vols, Harper Torchbooks, 1966) and the Catalogue of Roman novels on classical themes by W. B. Thompson (Dept. of Education, Leeds University).

Modern Works for Pupils:

Inside the Ancient World Series (Macmillan) especially:
R. Barrow: *Greek and Roman Education*
M. Massey and P. Moreland: *Slavery in Ancient Rome*
A. G. McKay: *Vitruvius, Architect and Engineer*
K. McLeish: *Roman Comedy*
D. Taylor: *Cicero and Rome*

Greek and Roman Topics Series (Allen & Unwin), especially:
K. McLeish: *Food and Drink*
J. Murrell: *Athletics, Sports and Games*
D. Taylor: *Acting and the Stage*
D. Taylor: *Work in Ancient Greece and Rome*

Cambridge Schools Classics Project: Roman materials (valuable sources from Roman Empire), C.U.P.

Aspects of Roman Life, Longman (for younger children): (ed. P. Hodge)
The Roman House
Roman Towns
Roman Family Life
Roman Sport and Entertainment

Cambridge Introduction to the History of Mankind (C.U.P.):
I. Andrews: *Pompeii*
T. Cairns: *The Romans and Their Empire*
J. Wilkes: *The Roman Army*

J. A. Harrison: *Roman Education*, Bell, 1978
K. McLeish and R. Nichols: *Through Roman Eyes*, Cambridge, 1976

Recent books of reference – often suitable for older pupils, many very well illustrated:

GENERAL

J. P. V. D. Balsdon: *Life and Leisure In Ancient Rome*, The Bodley Head, 1969
J. Carcopino: *Daily Life in Ancient Rome*, (tr. H. T. Rowell), Penguin Books, 1956
F. R. Cowell: *Everyday Life in Ancient Rome*, Batsford, 1961
L. Friedlander: *Roman Life and Manners Under the Early Empire*, (tr. L. A. Magnus and J. H. Freese), London, 1907
U. E. Paoli: *Rome: Its People Life and Customs* (tr. R. D. McNaughten), Longman, 1963.

M. Brion: *Pompeii and Herculaneum: The Glory and the Grief*, London, 1960
L. B. Dal Maso: *Rome of the Caesars* (tr. M. Hollingsworth), Bonechi-Edizoni
J. J. Deiss: *Herculaneum*, London & New York, 1966
D. R. Dudley: *Urbs Roma*, London, 1967
M. Grant: *The Roman Forum*, Spring Books, 1974
M. Grant: *Cities of Vesuvius*, Spring Books, 1974
R. Meiggs: *Roman Ostia*, Oxford, 1960

J. H. d'Arms: *Romans on the Bay of Naples*, Harvard, 1971
L. Casson: *Travel in the Ancient World*, Allen & Unwin, 1974
K. D. White: *Agricultural Implements of the Roman World*, London, 1974
K. D. White: *Roman Farming*, London, 1970

A. G. McKay: *Greek and Roman Domestic Architecture*, London, 1972
J. Percival: *The Roman Villa*, Batsford, 1976

A. H. Duff: *Freedmen in the Early Roman Empire*, Oxford, 1928
R. MacMullen: *Roman Social Relations*, London, 1974
A. N. Sherwin-White: *The Roman Citizenship*, Oxford, 1973
S. Treggiari: *Roman Freedmen in the Late Republic*, Oxford, 1969

G. Picard: *Roman Painting*, London, 1970
M. Wheeler: *Roman Art and Architecture*, Thames & Hudson, 1964

J. Lindsay: *The Writing on the Wall*, London, 1960

S. Bonner: *Education in Ancient Rome*, Methuen, 1977

J. A. Crook: *Law and Life of Rome*, Thames & Hudson, 1967

W. Beare: *The Roman Stage*, Methuen, 1969
G. E. Duckworth: *The Nature of Roman Comedy*, Princeton, 1952
F. H. Sandbach: *The Comic Theatre of Greece and Rome*, Chatto & Windus, 1977

M. Grant: *Gladiators*, Penguin Books, 1971
J. Pearson: *Arena*, Thames and Hudson, 1973

A. Cameron: *Circus Factions*, Oxford, 1976

J. P. V. D. Balsdon: *Roman Women*, The Bodley Head, 1962

C. Mosse: *The Ancient World at Work*, Chatto & Windus, 1969
H. Tanzer: *The Common People of Pompeii*, Baltimore, 1939

R. M. Ogilvie: *The Romans and Their Gods*, Chatto & Windus, 1969
F. H. Sandbach: *The Stoics*, Chatto & Windus, 1975

Index